THE
POCKET BOOK
OF
LIVERPOOL

By Leo Moynihan

To Catherine and Daisy,
my home's Gerrard and Torres

Published by Vision Sports Publishing in 2010

Vision Sports Publishing
19-23 High Street
Kingston upon Thames
Surrey
KT1 1LL

www.visionsp.co.uk

Text © Leo Moynihan
Illustrations © Bob Bond
Sporting Caricatures

ISBN: 978-1905326-91-4

Series editor: Jim Drewett
Series production: Martin Cloake
Design: Neal Cobourne
Illustrations: Bob Bond
Cover photography: Paul Downes, Objective Image
All pictures: Getty Images

Printed and bound in China by Toppan Printing Co Ltd

A CIP catalogue record for this book is available from the British Library

THIS IS AN UNOFFICIAL PUBLICATION

All statistics in *The Pocket Book of Liverpool* are correct up until the
end of the 2009/10 season.

CONTENTS

BOB PAISLEY

FOREWORD BY
IAN CALLAGHAN

Like so many young kids back in Liverpool in the 1950s I used to cherish going to Anfield. I'd go in the Boys Pen and what I can remember most was the sense of anticipation every time Billy Liddell got the ball. What a player he was. Little did I know that I would one day replace him in the team.

Bill Shankly saw something in the club and turned it into something brilliant and to this day, even the very young fans are fascinated by us older players and never tire of reading and hearing about the classic nights at Anfield or the wonderful players who graced that famous pitch.

The buzz when you used to run out in front of that crowd will never leave me and it just seemed so right that those fans were rewarded with success. I started out in the Second Division, won the League and was involved in 1964, when the club travelled to Reykjavik for its first ever match in Europe. I didn't even know where Reykjavik was but it was all so exciting. It may not have been the most important game in the club's long history but it was one I am so proud to have been involved in as it was the start of an incredible journey. When the whistle went in Rome in 1977 and we had been crowned champions of Europe my mind went back to that night in Iceland and just how far the club had come.

For me it was all made possible thanks to the two greatest managers that ever graced the game, Bill Shankly and then Bob Paisley – they were incredible men. Their enthusiasm, their knowledge and their expertise made it all possible and it was such a pleasure to play football. Both remain ingrained in the very fabric of the club and will never be forgotten. That's why it's such a pleasure to be involved with this book that celebrates not only those two greats but also so many others who have helped make Liverpool FC what it is today.

I remain a massive fan and was as pleased as anyone to see Jamie Carragher beat my all-time European appearances record recently. He's a local lad and a fantastic player and it's so exciting to see new chapters in the club's history being played out in front of me. I've told him though that he'll do well to beat my overall appearance record!

Today I make the journey to Anfield for every home match and I still get the buzz in my stomach that I used to back in the 1950s on my way to see Billy Liddell. I have supported and played for the most fantastic club in the world and have loved every minute of it.

Ian Callaghan

...CLUB DIRECTORY...

Club address: Anfield Stadium,
Liverpool, L4 0TH
Telephone: 0151 263 2361
Club Customer Services:
  0844 844 2005 (UK),
  0044 (0) 870 220 2345 (non-UK)
Ticket Sales, Credit-Card hotline:
  0844 844 0844 (UK)
  0044 (0) 870 220 2151 (non-UK)
Club Superstore: 0151 264 2300
Liverpool Soccer Schools: 0151 477 1201
Official membership Dept: 0844 499 3000
LFC Official Magazine: 0845 143 0001

Club Website:

www.liverpoolfc.tv

Mail Order UK:

0870 111 8107;

Hillsborough:

Hillsborough Family Support Group,

69 Anfield Road, Liverpool, L4 0TH

Email: info@hfsg.co.uk

Hillsborough Justice Campaign:

178 Walton Breck Road,

Liverpool, L4 0RG

Tel: 0151 2605262

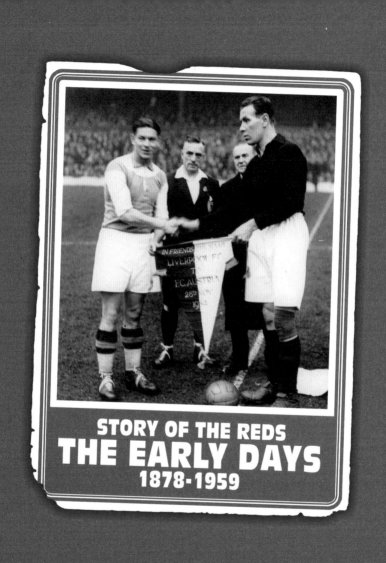

STORY OF THE REDS
THE EARLY DAYS
1878-1959

"The Liverpool Club is sure to prosper..."

Notes in the match programme from Liverpool FC's first ever match, 1st September 1892

With winter turning to spring in the March of 1892, local businessman, tycoon and wannabe football club owner John Houlding prepared his home at No. 73 Anfield Road for a small but vital meeting. Little did he know that what would happen in that red-bricked building would one day reverberate around the footballing world.

Little did he know that the fruit of his gathering would one day be known wherever the game is played and enjoyed. From the favelas of Brazil to the paddy-fields of China, Liverpool Football Club has become synonymous with passion, glory and excellence but, as Houlding straightened his tie and preened his moustache whilst awaiting those guests, the idea that any football club would one day exist was far from certain.

Everton FC (originally St Domingo FC) had been formed in 1878 and Houlding had taken an active interest, negotiating a new home ground in Anfield when the already successful club had to move from its Stanley Park pitch in 1883. The club boomed, attracting sizable support and won its first Championship in 1891.

That very year, Houlding had bought the Anfield ground for himself and had begun to exert his authority on the club and its members. Those men held strong Methodist beliefs and mistrusted their landlord and his methods. Houlding had made his fortune from the brewery business and, despite his philanthropy and many charitable considerations, was seen by many Everton members as a ringleader in the drunken circus that was urban Victorian England. The fact that the Everton players had to get changed in Houlding's pub over the road from the ground must have particularly grated with those Evertonian puritanicals.

Swashbuckling captain Alex Raisbeck led the club to its first League title

To be fair, Houlding had been bankrolling the club for many years, paying their rent, building grandstands, and looking after travel costs. No matter, he was a figure of disrepute and when he proposed a rise in rent from £100 per annum to £250, the storm clouds began to hover. Houlding offered to sell Anfield to its members (at a very tidy profit to himself) but they declined, refusing even to meet his rent demands.

Houlding, far from being seen as a man whose vision and capital had put the new club on the

The 1905/06 side with the League trophy (on the left), the Liverpool Cup and the enormous Sheriff of London Charity Shield

road to success, was instead painted as the villain; an opportunist looking out for his own fat wallet. On March 12th he got wind of a meeting being held by the club's hierarchy and turned up unannounced. He argued his case and left, officially no longer part of the club.

He had just 19 allies out of the club's 279 members,
three of the first team squad and a ground. The will of
that breakaway party meant that a new team would be
formed; a team that would have to attract support away
from Everton and inspire the whole city and so, on
15th March 1892, Liverpool Football club was born.

Houlding pumped money into the club but more importantly hired football men such as William Barclay and John McKenna. 'Directors' by title but really joint managers they would win the Lancashire League in the first season and the Second Division in their second.

The club's formative seasons saw them promoted and relegated twice before 1896 when, with the appointment of new coach Tom Watson, they finally got the hang of the top tier. Sporting a new red kit for the 1898/99 season, Liverpool finished second but in 1900/01, thanks largely to their blond swashbuckling captain Alex Raisbeck (think Hyppia with a tache!) they could for the first time call themselves Champions of England.

The title was won again in 1905/06 but a new maximum wage of £4 a week hindered the hitherto generous payers at Anfield and mediocrity followed. A first ever Cup Final appearance in 1914 gave the travelling fans (even then they were a large and vociferous bunch) a trip to London but their side was beaten 1-0 by Burnley.

When football resumed in 1919 after the war, the club were able to help get life back on track. Back-to-back titles were won in 1922 and 1923 with a side inspired by the free-scoring Harry Chambers and the always popular Ulsterman and goalkeeper Elisha Scott.

Football, though, was changing. Herbert Chapman at Huddersfield and later Arsenal was making the

Record signing Albert Stubbins cleans his boots at home the day after the deal was done in 1946 game a chess-like tactical battle and other managers struggled to keep up. Matt McQueen and later George Patterson at Anfield were keen scholars but couldn't live with Chapman when it came to the game's subtleties.

In 1936 Liverpool appointed George Kay, who set about building a better club. War once more pushed the game to the margins but on its return for the 1946/47 season Kay's Liverpool were crowned Champions. Billy Liddell, Albert Stubbins and a quiet defender named Bob Paisley were the heartbeat of an honest side but that league success was only followed up by an FA Cup final defeat to Arsenal in 1950.

Kay's health suffered and the following year he retired, replaced by Don Welsh. Liverpool struggled. New faces failed to gel and older faces looked, well, old. In 1954 the club were relegated. Welsh was sacked in 1956 but new boss Phil Taylor didn't fare better. Season after season, promotion back to the First Division seemed like a step too far for this well-supported but ultimately underachieving football club.

They housed a great in Billy Liddell, they bought a future great in Roger Hunt in 1959, but that same year they were knocked out of the cup by non-league Worcester. Phil Taylor would step down in the November citing the pressures of the job and for two weeks the club struggled without a manager as a frantic board muddled over applications for the Anfield helm.

What was needed was a man who could steady the ship, a man who knew his stuff and who could turn what had become a dreary, uninspiring place full circle and make them great. At the beginning of December, the club and its fans got exactly that and much, much more. They got Bill Shankly and things would never be the same again.

Speedy outside left Billy Liddell in action in 1949

BADGE OF
HONOUR

> "A Liver bird upon my chest
> We are the men, of Shankly's best
> A team that plays the Liverpool way
> And wins the Championship in May"
>
> Liverpool fans song

It's late May 2005. Of the thousands of Liverpool flags and banners which blanketed the city of Istanbul like some sort of eerie red mist swept in from The Bosporus, one remains in the memory. *Another Great Night Out With My Bird* said it all.

The first permanent shirt badge, introduced in 1957

The bird in question was of course the Liver Bird, a mythical beast but one that has travelled all over Europe, becoming a very real symbol of glory.

In fact, go anywhere in the world where the game of football is loved, be it in a Buenos Aires steakhouse or a Tokyo karaoke bar, show them a picture of a Liver Bird and the response will be, "Liverpool Football Club".

The bird itself has been spreading those wings and chewing on that vegetation for far longer than man has been cheering on the game of football. There are many schools of thought about the origins of this creature, dating back to the 13th century, but over the ages it came to firmly represent a city itself growing in

stature and importance. Soon two metal birds were overlooking the river Mersey on top of the Liver Buildings, where they remain to this day.

By 1892 when John Houlding started his very own football club, he was looking to outdo his old team, Everton. The name Liverpool gave his team a broader appeal and so it made sense if a symbol for the club was to be chosen that it should represent the city as a whole.

In 1901 – the year the club won its first league title – the bird was adopted as the club badge but while she regularly appeared on matchday programmes, she wouldn't actually appear on the shirt for nearly 50 years. Kits up to and into the 1950s wouldn't include club emblems, but exceptions were made

In 1970, a stripped down image was stitched into the famous red shirt

The bird flew high over Wembley for the first time in 1965

for special occasions. Liverpool played Arsenal in the 1950 FA Cup final and although they had to play in their white away strip they did proudly wear the Liver Bird on their left breasts. The game finished 2-0 to the Gunners, fuelling the Evertonian gag about the Liverpudlian who saved up for the day that his side won the cup and died a millionaire.

Cruel jokes continued into the decade but the plain red tops changed in 1957 when a permanent badge – a white oval shape with the red bird and the letters LFC - was included on the strip.

The bird went yellow between 1976 and 1984

In 1965 the bird made its way to Wembley for yet another Cup final but those Everton clowns were still joking, insisting their rivals would only win the cup when the Liver Birds flew away from the Liver Building. Oddly they were right as on that famous day when Ron Yeats lifted the trophy the two birds had been taken from the building to be cleaned.

A shield housed the bird for the first time in 1987 in a revamped but still simple design

In 1970 the surrounding oval was

removed from the crest with the bird now standing alone above LFC. Prior to the glorious 1976/77 season, the bird was changed from white to yellow and that's how it would stay until 1985 when it went back to white. In 1987, the bird was placed on a shield, whilst underneath Liverpool Football Club replaced LFC.

It was for the 1992/93 campaign – the club's 100th – that the badge was altered to its current state. The shield holding the bird remained but above it were now the Shankly Gates with the words "You'll Never Walk Alone". Below the shield EST.1892 symbolised the relevant date and on each side was an eternal flame symbolising the Hillsborough memorial at Anfield.

The current badge, introduced in 1992, is heavy with symbolism

That famous bird remains firmly on her perch, not only at the top of the game but on a shirt made famous by the football club she represents. It is only right and fitting though that she is joined by the memory of Bill Shankly – the man who made it all possible – and the 96 fans who lost their lives supporting the team they so dearly loved.

THE KOP

What started out as a huge, sprawling mass of soil and cinders would, over decades, transform itself into much more than merely a terrace on which to observe football. The Spion Kop and those who stood – or now sit – on it have become the stuff of legend.

The Kop itself was a gift to the fans from the club. In 1906, Liverpool were crowned League Champions for the second time and the ground's average gate of 18,000, while not bad, was not all it could be. The majority of fans chose to stand at one of the modest terraces on either the Anfield Road or Walton Breck Road ends of the ground.

That summer the club built a vast terrace at the Walton Breck site and while it was hardly a feat of engineering – it had no roof and just a small white picket fence at its bottom – it did offer a great view and got off to a winning start on 1st September 1906 when Stoke City were beaten 1-0 in heatwave conditions.

Originally known as the Oakfield Road Embankment, it needed something catchier. Spioenkop was a hill in South Africa that had witnessed one of the recent Boer War's most bloody battles. In January 1900 British and Boer troops clashed and 300 Lancashire Fusiliers (heavily recruited from the Merseyside area) lay dead.

Ernest Edwards, a local sports journalist, suggested that the new terrace pay homage to those who died and so Anfield now housed The Spion Kop.

Mighty Mouse takes a bow on the famous terrace in 1976

After the Great War and with Liverpool winning back-to-back titles in the early 1920s, Anfield regularly enjoyed 50,000-plus crowds and so in 1928 a new, improved Kop was opened, the biggest of its kind anywhere in the country. It was expanded to now house 28,000 spectators, it measured 425 x 131 feet and more importantly had a vast cantilever roof that amplified the roars of what was by now a vociferous support.

The years up to and following the Second World War saw no let up in the popularity of either the Kop or the reputation it was getting for its noise and humour. One man, invited to Anfield in the 1950s, sat in the directors' box and rather than watching much of the match, his eyes feasted on the famous terrace and he fantasised about how special it would be to send a team out every other week to play for them. That man was Bill Shankly.

The Scot soon got his wish and with his team

blossoming into one of the best around, the Kop's notoriety grew and grew. In April 1964, with Liverpool needing to beat Arsenal at Anfield to win the title, BBC's *Panorama* sent a camera crew to the ground to study the all-swaying, all-singing Kop who didn't need asking twice to put on a show. The reporter was awestruck but managed to put it into words.

"It used to be thought that the Welsh international rugby crowds were the most musical and passionate in the world, but I've never seen anything like this Liverpool crowd…The Duke of Wellington before the battle of Waterloo said of his own troops, 'I don't know what they do to the enemy, but by God they frighten me.' I'm sure some of the players in today's match will be feeling the same way."

Just moments before a European Cup quarter-final with Cologne in 1965, the match was postponed due to heavy snow. With the Kop packed, its cold inhabitants took to the pitch and started a snowball fight that escalated into a running battle with those fans at the Anfield Road end and viewed by Shankly and his players who had ringside seats!

Such camaraderie with the rest of the ground was

In front of the famous old stand, a new generation acclaims the team after the 2005 European Cup victory

highlighted on one foggy night when Liverpool scored at the opposite end of the ground. The Kop, blighted by the fog sang, "Who scored the goal?" The Anfield Road fans obliged by shouting back "Tony Hateley"!

In 1994, the Kop as a terrace closed. The last match was a 1-0 defeat to Norwich but the day was all about the fans ("they did their bit, we didn't do ours" said Ian Rush after the match). As a vast seating area (it today holds over 12,000) it remains as famous as it ever has been, with even supporters of clubs who play their football at shrines to the game like the Nou Camp or the Bernabéu pleased to have said they have seen it after a special night at Anfield.

Deafening songs, an unforgiving wit (a favourite is when John Wark took the ball fully in the groin and finally got up with the Kop singing his name in high-pitched tones), a vast knowledge for the game and an unparralled sense of fair-play (away goalkeepers have been applauded

The Kop in full voice, still one of the most stirring sights and sounds in the game

for years and even Arsenal players were in shock when in 1989 they snatched the league with their last-minute winner only to be clapped off by a packed Kop) are all evident on the famous terrace that has become known as the world's best "twelfth man".

ANFIELD

"I always thought that Anfield was a place more beautiful than Heaven"

John Aldridge

You've had your pint(s), sung your pre-match songs and you're walking through the red-bricked terraced streets on your way to the match as the throng of fans begin to buzz with anticipation. You approach the stadium and the click-click-click of the turnstiles seem to be opening the butterfly cage in your stomach.

You walk up the steps and there it is; suddenly you catch sight of that pristine green pitch. It doesn't matter how many times you've done it, it's a wonderful moment. After all – as the sign in the players tunnel reminds us – THIS IS ANFIELD.

For 125 years fans have come to Anfield to watch the match. Things have changed of course. For starters those fans used to be Evertonians. The Blues moved to a site at Anfield due to the growing popularity of their games being played on Stanley Park.

Fences and a stand were erected around the site, the local Sandon Pub was used as the dressing-rooms and in 1884 the first game was staged with Everton beating Earlstown 5-0.

The popularity of the game was at fever-pitch and in 1886 the club's major financier, John Houlding, paid £64 for another stand to be built on the Kemlyn Road and by the end of the decade all four ends housed supporters. It was such an impressive arena that, in 1889, England played an international there in front of 6,000 people.

In 1892, the dispute between Houlding and Everton's unhappy members reached breaking point. Houlding started his own club (see *Story of the Reds*, page 9) and Anfield had proud new tenants.

The ground had suffered from the break-up, with many Evertonians removing fittings (including turnstiles) but Houlding wasn't one to stand still.

Liverpool's first game – a friendly against local side

Roger Hunt in action in 1968, a period in which Bill Shankly instigated major ground improvements

Higher Walton which they won 8-0 in front of 200 people – offered no hints of the glory that would one day follow. But slowly the club established itself and as league football commenced, notable improvements became apparent at the stadium.

In 1895, with the Second Division won, the club paid £1,000 to build what is today the main stand. It housed 3,000 spectators and stood for 75 years. In 1903, the Anfield Road stand was improved and in 1906, after Liverpool had won their second

Emlyn Hughes celebrates a goal in 1973, the year floodlights were added to the top of the Kemlyn Road stand

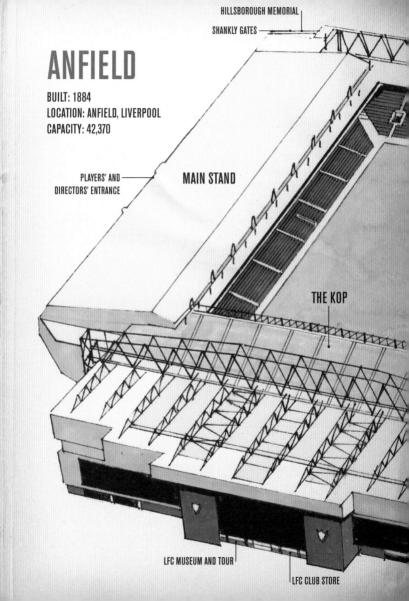

ANFIELD

BUILT: 1884
LOCATION: ANFIELD, LIVERPOOL
CAPACITY: 42,370

HILLSBOROUGH MEMORIAL

SHANKLY GATES

PLAYERS' AND
DIRECTORS' ENTRANCE

MAIN STAND

THE KOP

LFC MUSEUM AND TOUR

LFC CLUB STORE

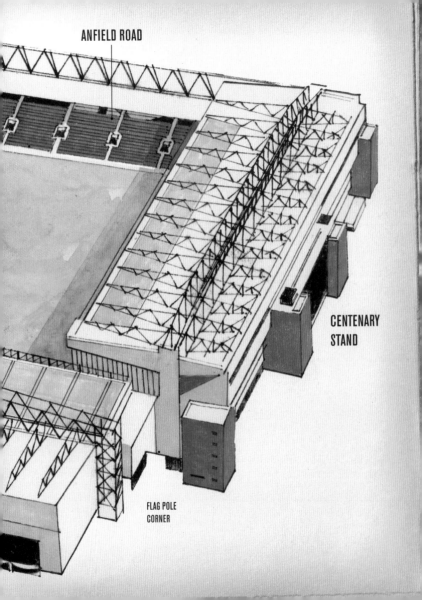

ANFIELD ROAD

CENTENARY
STAND

FLAG POLE
CORNER

The 1987 derby game is played out under a blood red sky

Championship, the fans were given a huge terrace that would be known as The Spion Kop. (See *The Kop*, page 24).

The barrel-roofed stand at the Kemlyn Road was also put up and Anfield was now one of the most impressive stadiums around.

The team that played there was just as exciting and after Championship seasons in the 1920s the Kop was extended to hold 30,000 people. With its new roof the imposing structure was now the largest covered stand in the country.

That same year the flag pole was erected on the corner of the Kop and Kemlyn Road stands. The pole was made from the mast of The Great Eastern, one of the first iron ships. After the ship was broken up at the docks, the mast was pulled up Everton Valley by horses. Today, Flag Pole Corner remains a notable part of the ground.

The ground remained untouched after the War, with significant chapters in its history being the record attendance of 61,905 that came to see a 1952 FA Cup tie against Wolves and the introduction of floodlights in 1957 at a cost of £12,000.

Two years after that, Bill Shankly arrived. Whilst he would shine more brightly than any floodlight ever could, he was by no means a fan of the stadium. Shankly had fallen in love with the people coming through the turnstiles but he immediately dubbed Anfield "The biggest toilet in Liverpool!"

So £350,000 was spent on a brand new Kemlyn Road stand and in 1965 (after the side's first FA Cup victory) the Anfield Road end was converted to a covered terrace.

Shortly after, plans to knock down the old main stand were approved and in March 1973 the Duke of Kent opened the modernised version that stands today. The new stand included floodlights along the roof. These were replicated along the Kemlyn Road stand (163 lights today light up the ground) which meant the end of the four pylons in each corner.

With European glory came further modification in the 1980s. The old Paddock in front of the main stand was seated in 1980, with the entire Anfield Road end following suit two years later.

The 26th August 1982 saw The Shankly Gates officially opened by the great man's wife Nessie in recognition of a manager who had helped make the place so special.

In 1992 the Kemlyn Road stand was demolished and replaced by The Centenary Stand that housed 11,000 seats and executive boxes.

Three years prior to that the Hillsborough disaster had effected all stadia but none more so than Anfield. Along with the permanent memorial and eternal flame situated next to The Shankly Gates, The Kop became an all-seated stand and opened in 1995, housing 13,000 fans.

The last major reconstruction of the famous place came in 1998. A second tier was added to the Anfield Road end but needed strengthening after Celtic fans complained of movement in the top tier during a testimonial for Ronnie Moran in 2000.

In 1999, just months after Bob Paisley's death, the club constructed gates in his name at the Kop Stand on Walton Breck Road.

Anfield remains one of the world's special footballing auditoriums. Ask the St Etienne and Chelsea players who had to contend with the atmosphere generated there in 1977 and 2005 respectively and they will talk of quite terrifying nights.

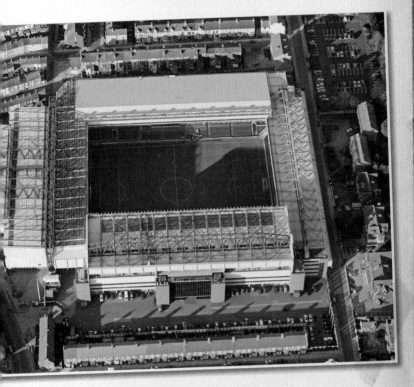

There are plans to build a new arena in the near future. Talk of progress and competing with the club's rivals will appease some but the sadness felt the day any move actually happens will be impossible to quantify. Bill Shankly himself once said, "The very word Anfield means more to me than I can describe." If he couldn't do it, who can?

A modern arena in the traditional British setting, hemmed in by terraced housing

GREAT GOALS

KEVIN KEEGAN
1974 FA CUP FINAL V NEWCASTLE

A confident Newcastle team had been put to the sword. Arguably the most one-sided second half in Cup Final history was drawing to an end and for the hordes of fans from Merseyside it was party time.

His team were 2-0 up and playing with a swagger but Bill Shankly was still dictating their actions, his hand movements insisting that the team play as a team. There was to be no late individual showboating.

"The Socialism I believe in is everyone working together, everyone having a share of the rewards," he once said. "It's the way I see football, the way I see life."

With two minutes remaining, the goalkeeper Ray Clemence held the ball. What followed was everything that Shankly held dear. After six passes out of defence the ball reached Kevin Keegan on the left-wing who had the vision to switch the play to Tommy Smith at right back.

Smith played a one-two with Brian Hall, another with Steve Heighway and from the byline played the ball across the goal for Keegan who had ghosted into the box to knock it into an empty net.

It was an ecstatic moment but it might go some way to explaining why - just two months later - Bill Shankly resigned. Having his seen his players encapsulate everything he wanted from the game, maybe the great man wondered if there was anywhere higher he could go.

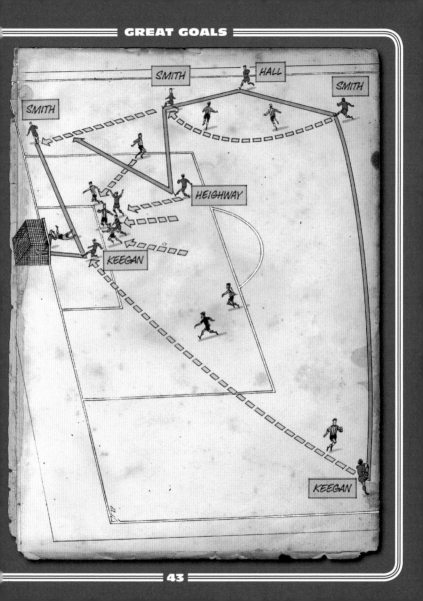

SMITH
HALL
SMITH
SMITH
HEIGHWAY
KEEGAN
KEEGAN

TERRY MCDERMOTT
1978 DIVISION ONE V TOTTENHAM

Tottenham had arrived at Anfield, newly promoted and full of early season confidence. Who could blame them?

Over the summer they had signed two of Argentina's World Cup winning squad but even with Ricardo Villa and Osvaldo Ardiles in their side, the Londoners could do nothing against a Liverpool team that would rampage its way to the league title.

A Dalglish brace, two more from David Johnson and one apiece from Ray Kennedy and Phil Neal saw the Reds six up when, with 76 minutes gone, the visitors won a corner. They must have savoured the respite but instead as Clemence claimed the cross and apparently harmlessly tossed it to Ray Kennedy, they were about to be ceremoniously taken apart once more.

Kennedy nudged the ball to Dalglish who fed Johnson just to the right of the centre circle. The striker in turn spotted the hare-like Steve Heighway down the left wing and sprayed the ball into his path. Spurs, like a discarded sandwich at the mercy of red ants, were helpless. Heighway played the perfect first time cross to the back post where Terry McDermott, who had sprinted the length of the field, headed past Barry Daines. "Probably the best goal in the history of the club," said Bob Paisley.

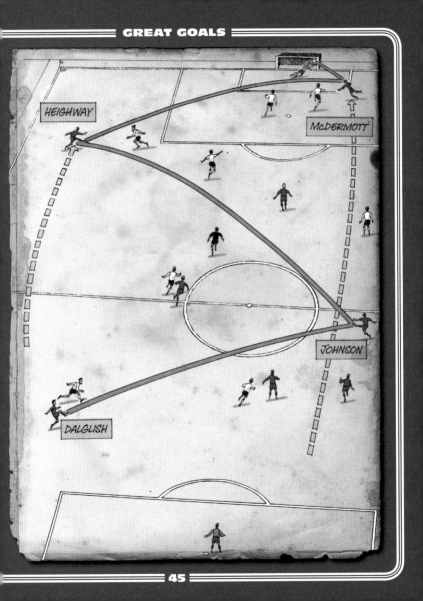

KENNY DALGLISH
1983 DIVISION ONE V ARSENAL

On the evening of the 10th September 1983, *Match of the Day* viewers settled into their armchairs to watch Liverpool's visit to Arsenal.

As Ian Rush collected the ball midway in his hosts' half and played the ball out to Sammy Lee on the right, the commentator John Motson told his audience that "[Liverpool] seem to find angles that other teams don't appreciate". What followed was an example of just how right the BBC man was as Liverpool cut through Arsenal's rearguard, making it all look so deliciously easy.

Craig Johnston had given Joe Fagan's men the lead in the first-half and in the 67th minute the game was over. Lee played it to Dalglish and then moved to receive the return pass from the striker, before spotting the run of Michael Robinson. A well-paced pass sent the former Brighton man towards the byline, before he back-heeled it to Dalglish who had run into the box.

Arsenal were firmly up against the ropes as Dalglish instinctively dummied his way past Graham Rix, took a touch and with his left foot curled a wonderful shot into Pat Jennings's top right-hand corner. The smile that followed said it all. No need for a finger gesture to silence the home crowd, no need for a hand cupped sarcastically around the ear. Dalglish just offered that huge grin that spoke of a man simply doing what he loved.

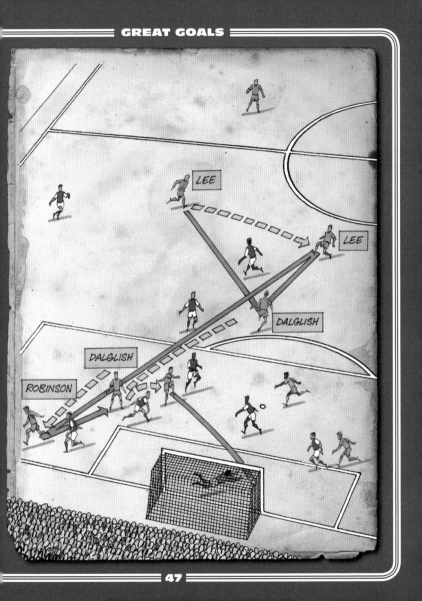

IAN RUSH
1986 FA CUP FINAL V EVERTON

It was a goal that won his club the FA Cup, won his club their first League and Cup double and had Evertonians everywhere cursing the day he was given football boots. It was also a goal that might have cost the striker a bit of cash.

Having taken Ronnie Whelan's pass down with a perfect first touch, Rush had slammed the ball past Bobby Mimms into the net, smashing a very carelessly placed camera as he did so. "The photographer actually sent me a bill," laughs Rush. "I got back for pre-season and there was this bill for the damage caused. Someone at Anfield paid it I think. I didn't. He left his camera in the goal, what did he think might happen?"

Everton had led but after going 2-1 down replaced their right back Gary Stevens with Adrian Heath, a striker. Unfortunately for the Toffees, this was a Liverpool team capable of exploiting such a punt.

Johnston and Rush had combined well in their own half before the ball reached Jan Molby in the centre-circle. The Great Dane simply but brilliantly laid the ball off into the space now vacated by Stevens, and Ronnie Whelan was marauding toward the box. With his player-manager Kenny Dalglish using all his wily experience with a decoy run to his left, Whelan looked up and chipped a delicate pass to Rush. Like that camera, Everton's hopes were in pieces.

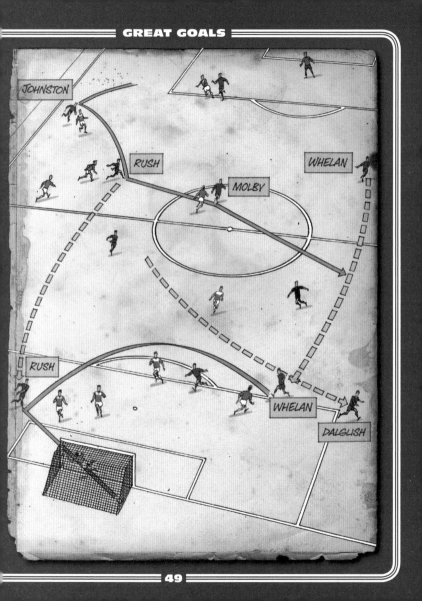

JOHN BARNES
1987 DIVISION ONE V QUEENS PARK RANGERS

Amazingly there were still a few sceptics. Anfield had been closed for the start of the 1987/88 campaign and whilst travelling reds had come home from London and Coventry with tales of the new star in their new team, some had their doubts.

Even virtuoso performances in the subsequent home games had the more old-school fans merely impressed rather than convinced that John Barnes was the real deal. He wasn't a Liverpool player, they claimed. He was too individualistic, nowhere near the team player that past success had been built upon. Then QPR came to town and by 4.45pm, the sceptics had gone.

The Londoners were top of the table (albeit Liverpool had games in hand) but were taken apart by Kenny Dalglish's men at their fluid, awesome best. Barnes had already got a goal to help put Liverpool 3-0 up with five minutes left, but the Reds were not done. QPR's Kevin Brock stepped across the halfway line but was tackled by Barnes, proving anyone who thought he wouldn't work as well as thrill very wrong indeed.

He bore down on the Rangers defence and with all the balance of a downhill skier slalomed between the centre halves before slotting it past David Seaman. And with that the whole Kop had a new hero.

BEARDSLEY

BARNES

BARNES

ROBBIE FOWLER
1997 CUP WINNERS' CUP V SK BRANN

To a set of fans so accustomed to a glut of silverware, it would be safe to say that the 1990s was a hard decade for Reds. Thank heavens then for Robbie Fowler.

The emergence of this local hero was like their own big, shiny trophy to fans desperate for new heroes to embrace and on this night in Norway the Toxteth striker gave an insight into just how exciting a player he was.

The quarter-final first leg of the 1997 Cup Winners' Cup may not take pride of place in the annuls of the club's great European nights but with just ten minutes gone, this was Fowler at his ridiculously raw best.

Neil Ruddock launched one of his thumping left-footers from defence to Stig Inge Bjornebye tight on the left-wing and the full-back cushioned a header that dropped behind the onrushing Fowler.

What happened next was the work of a street footballer, a player as happy to smash a ball against a garage door in the name of a goal.

As the ball dropped behind him, Fowler flicked it over his and his static marker's heads with his left foot, ran on into the box and – amidst the admiring cooing of the home crowd – slammed it past the somewhat awestruck Norwegian keeper.

FOWLER

FOWLER

BJORNEBYE

RUDDOCK

STEVEN GERRARD
2004 CHAMPIONS LEAGUE GROUP STAGES V OLYMPIAKOS

To a generation of young Liverpool fans, the notion that events on the Anfield pitch could actually rock the famous arena to its very foundations were the stuff of legend. They would happily listen - albeit enviously - to their elders' tales of Inter Milan in 1965 or St Etienne in 1977, but they were yet to have their own "I was there" moment. Step in Steven Gerrard, a man desperate to ensure that the club, his club, continued to fill their history books with glorious pages.

The day before this vital final group game, Gerrard had said he didn't want to wake up in the UEFA Cup. With just four minutes left though, that's exactly where he was heading. Rivaldo had given the Greek side a first-half lead, meaning that Liverpool had to score three goals to progress. Florent Sinama Pongolle had put them back in it immediately after the re-start and with 12 minutes left another substitute, Neil Mellor, had scrambled one in to give the team hope.

The Kop willed the team forward. Jamie Carragher cleverly kept possession, resisting the temptation of just launching it into the box. Instead he picked out Mellor who cushioned a header down to the onrushing and eager Gerrard. Up stepped the skipper and in a thunderous flash, the ball was spinning wonderfully in the Greek net.

MELLOR

CARRAGHER

GERRARD

RED EUROPE

> "This is the second time I've beaten the Germans here... the first time was in 1944. I drove into Rome on a tank when the city was liberated."

Bob Paisley after Liverpool's 1977 European Cup win against Borussia Moenchengladbach in Rome

On his arrival at Anfield in 1959, Bill Shankly had clear intentions. "My idea was to build Liverpool into a bastion of invincibility," he later said. "Napoleon had that idea and he conquered the bloody world!"

Forty years, three UEFA Cups and five European Cups later and Shanks can be satisfied that his idea bore fruit. The first manoeuvres into Europe came in August 1964 against the minnows of KR Reykjavik, and an 11-1 aggregate win.

Defeat to Inter Milan in the semi-final was followed by another loss the following year, this time Borussia Dortmund in the Cup Winners' Cup final at Glasgow's Hampden Park.

Six years later and Liverpool had their first European trophy under Shankly when the UEFA Cup was won against Borussia Moenchengladbach. The same trophy was won in 1976, this time with Bob Paisley at the helm and Bruges the defeated opponents.

These two clubs would be lucky omens for Paisley's sides. In 1977, the Germans were beaten in Rome where Liverpool lifted their first European Cup, successfully defending it the very next year against the Belgians, this time at Wembley.

Rome 1977 is especially evocative for Reds everywhere, even those not born then who listen eagerly to stories of 30,000 Scousers making their way to the Eternal City by any means necessary.

In 1981, it was Paris's turn to welcome the famous travelling fans who went insane by the Seine after Alan Kennedy's late winner against Real Madrid. Paisley became the first (and hitherto only) man to win the trophy three times but two years later passed the mantle to Joe Fagan who, in his first season, went back to Rome and orchestrated another win, this time against Roma.

The tragedy of Heysal in 1985 destroyed the club's reputation and its once perfect standing in the game. For

Celebrating the 1984 European Cup win after Roma were beaten 4-2 on penalties in the Eternal City

six years they would be banned from the European game and throughout the 1990s struggled to find their feet on the continent.

In 2001 though, under Gerard Houllier, Liverpool made their way back into the elite with a dramatic 5-4 win in the UEFA Cup final over Alaves in Dortmund. Symbolically, UEFA awarded the club's fans a fair-play award for their behaviour. The club had come full circle.

Four years later and in their thousands those same supporters followed Rafa Benitez's team to Istanbul for a night no one will ever forget. In 2007 they did the same, this time to Athens and without the win, but the club and its supporters remain among ... elite and

LONDON 1978

PARI 1981

WHERE THE CUPS WERE WON

MONCHENGLADBACH 1973

DORTMUND 2001

ROME 1977 & 1984

ISTANBUL 2005

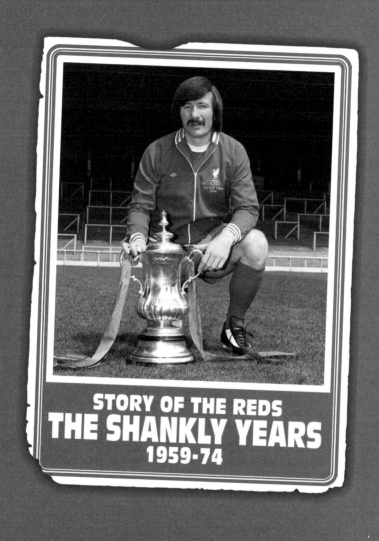

STORY OF THE REDS
THE SHANKLY YEARS
1959-74

> ## "I want to build a team that's invincible, so that they have to send a team from bloody Mars to beat us"
>
> Bill Shankly

When it happened it was a modest affair. There was no glitzy press conference, no 24-hour analysis. Just a simple statement from the club Chairman, Tom Williams: "Of the small number who came up to the requirements, the board decided to ascertain the position of Mr W. Shankly, now with Huddersfield Town, and eventually offered the management to him. He put the position before his board and, after expressing their regret at the prospect of losing his services, they have agreed that Mr Shankly shall join Liverpool FC."

So there it was. Mr W. Shankly had "come up to the requirements". Those requirements must have been to turn his new employers from Second Division also-rans into one of the greatest clubs in Europe, to produce a brand of flowing and effervescent football well worthy of a city soon to be awash with Merseybeat, and to give the Liverpool people who would flock to Anfield in their tens of thousands the time of their lives, because that's exactly what he managed to do.

Bill Shankly was only 46 years old when he arrived

Likely lads Ian St John and Tommy Smith at the club photocall in 1965

at Liverpool and his youthful enthusiasm was exactly what the club needed. The Ayrshire man had no plans to completely shake up the place. He recognised that the men behind the scenes were potential wells of knowledge. The trainers at the club, Bob Paisley, Joe Fagan and Rueben Bennett, were kept on to work with him but as his first game in charge proved, there was much work to be done.

A 4-0 home defeat to Cardiff City showed no signs of the glory to come but it was to be the last match for which the Liverpool side was picked by a selection committee. Shankly wanted full control of the team and he got it. Youngsters such as Gerry

Champions 1966: (Back)
Strong, Lawler, Lawrence,
Byrne, Smith. (Front) Callaghan,
Hunt, Milne, Yeats, Thompson,
St John, Stevenson

Byrne and Ian Callaghan would become fixtures and Roger Hunt was clearly a star in waiting but otherwise, reinforcements were needed.

That wouldn't be easy because of a Liverpool board which had developed a reputation for being far from generous ("They'd complain about changing a light bulb" laughed Ian St John years later) and bids to sign a young Denis Law and Jack Charlton proved insufficient to secure the players' services. In the summer of 1961, after yet another promotion push had fallen just short, Eric Sawyer came to Anfield. It was a watershed arrival. The businessman's presence on the board gave Shankly an ally, a man who could put some hard cash behind the Scotsman's dream.

Immediately the club transfer record was broken with the £37,000 purchase of centre forward Ian St John from Motherwell. The club stayed north of the border to capture the big defender Ron Yeats from Dundee United. Shankly would later talk of his mission to "conquer the bloody world" and now he was mobilising his army.

His side were promoted as Champions in 1962 and there was a growing feeling among supporters that the wilderness years were truly coming to an end. Byrne, Gordon Milne, Yeats, Hunt, St John, Callaghan; these players who helped win promotion would soon take the club to further heights. It would all be orchestrated by Shankly and his incredible backroom staff, or "The Boot Room", as it would famously become known.

Beatlemania was sweeping the nation, but the red half of Liverpool also had a footballing Fab Four to get excited about. Shankly, the front man on lead vocals, brilliantly aided by a rhythm section of Paisley, Fagan and Bennett.

The club took stock in the top flight, brought more quality on board and, in 1963/64, were

Emlyn Hughes and Ray Clemence lift the 1974 FA Cup

The 1973 League Championship trophy is paraded in front of The Kop

crowned Champions. It was an incredible turnaround. Only five years earlier the club looked to have run aground, now they were sailing into the beautifully exciting waters of the European Cup.

In 1965, they would reach the semi-finals of Europe's top club competition only to lose in controversial fashion to Inter Milan. No matter, just days before the first leg, Liverpool had gone to Wembley and won the FA Cup for the first time, beating Leeds 2-1. It was a momentous occasion with North London awash in red and white.

The title was again won in 1966 to complete

an incredible three seasons, but that was to be the pinnacle of Shankly's first great team. St John, Hunt, Yeats et al would soldier on into the late 1960s but a Cup defeat at Watford in 1970 proved to Shankly that a new team had to be built if his "Bastion of invincibility" was to be realised.

Ray Clemence, Steve Heighway, John Toshack and Kevin Keegan all joined a young Emlyn Hughes and, despite a Cup Final defeat to Arsenal in 1970, the new team was about to embark upon a fresh era of dominance. The championship was won in 1972/73, as was their first European trophy after Borussia Monchengladbach were beaten in the UEFA Cup.

Keegan, a £33,000 steal from Scunthorpe, was playing his way to superstar status and the following season would see the FA Cup captured once more after a quite brilliant team performance against Newcastle finished 3-0 to the Reds. As the squad took its rightful plaudits around the old stadium, Shankly's team and his fortunes looked set in red stone.

Fans travelled back to Lime Street Station already dreaming of further great footballing days out. They'd travel the world to see Shankly's men in action but, on the 12th July 1974, the club called a press conference in which the Chairman John Smith announced the unthinkable: "It is with great regret, as chairman of the board, I have to inform you that Mr Shankly has intimated that he wishes to retire from league football".

And with that he was gone.

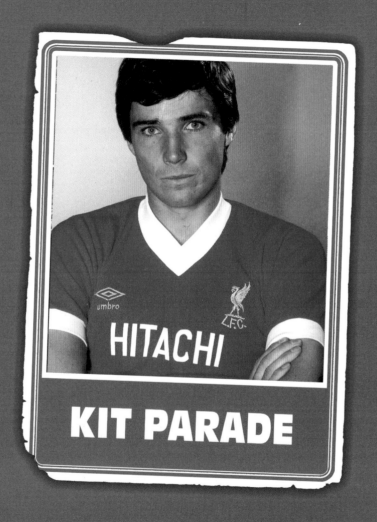

HITACHI

KIT PARADE

"Chairman Mao has never seen a greater show of red strength than today"

Bill Shankly after the 1974 FA Cup final win over Newcastle

Everton may have left Anfield in 1892, but the blue colours remained

Fans of every era and of every age will have indulged themselves with the same fantasy.

There they stand in the dressing-room, the crowd sing *You'll Never Walk Alone* whilst eagerly awaiting their arrival, and that famous red shirt is pulled over their head. It's a perfect fit and swells with pride as they touch the This Is Anfield sign and run onto the hallowed turf.

Down the years those daydreams will have included heading in a pinpoint Billy Liddell cross, playing a one-two with Kevin Keegan, latching onto a perfect Dalglish through-ball, or celebrating in front of a bouncing Kop with Gerrard and Torres.

The Liverpool shirt; to many of those fans it is as mythical as the Liver Bird that stands proudly upon it. Sure, designs change every other year and you can buy the replica in any store these days; you can even have your favourite star's name put on the back, but the thought of pulling the real one on come match day makes the red top something special.

Not that it was always red. In 1892, Anfield housed its new club and while many Evertonians helped themselves to some of its fixtures and fittings, the kit first worn by their side remained at the stadium. John Houlding wanted to move the club on but for now the pale blue and white halved tops would have to do.

In 1894, with promotion to the First Division secured, Liverpool opted for a new style, something to distinguish themselves from their neighbours. Everton had experimented with their own variations, including a ruby red strip, but they were keen to have their own royal blue. Liverpool therefore would go for red, and so the battle colours that would divide a city were born.

The red half of Liverpool were beginning to get the hang of the top flight and in 1901 the red tops (with

The modern strip, with distinctive V-neck, developed during the 1950s

three buttons), long white shorts and red socks were the uniform of champions.

The kit remained a constant until after the First World War when black socks were adopted to go with the 1920s style of a drawstring collar. Into the 1930s and the string was replaced with buttons; before the War, the socks were changed to red and white stripes.

It is said that as the War came to an end and Liverpool toured Germany to play the Combined Services, they were given a brand new and impressive set of red shirts. Materials were at a premium so they gladly accepted but it later transpired that the kit – a red buttoned V-neck – was made from discarded Nazi flags pulled down by the conquering allies. Wherever they came from, they worked as that next season, Liverpool won the league!

Liverpool also had a white away strip. The top had red collars, the shorts were black and the socks red with two white hoops, a style of away kit that would be copied over the years. The 1950s were far from inspiring on the pitch but saw the birth of the more modern strip, including the crest regularly on the shirt and,

All-red was adopted in 1964, with this version worn to win the European Cup in 1977

toward the latter stages of the decade, the distinctive V-neck. The white shorts now sported a red stripe along the outside whilst the socks remained hooped. The away kit also remained white with a red V-neck, the shorts were black and the socks now white.

Then came Bill Shankly and everything would change. The Scot had already revolutionised the team, making them champions of England in 1964 (by now the V-neck had become a round neck) but as they made their first foray into Europe the following season, the quite sartorial Shankly had thoughts about a change in the colour scheme.

It was November of 1964, Anderlecht were to be the visitors to Anfield and Shankly had been curious to try something new. After training he had called over his massive skipper, Ron Yeats and with his staff watched as Yeats tried on a new all red kit and ran out from the Anfield tunnel.

Now the 6ft 2in Yeats – a former abattoir slaughterman from Aberdeen – would have looked intimidating

The speckling on the 1989 shirt was an acquired taste

in a tutu but Shankly saw something in the all red, something powerful that would frighten the opposition. That night – after his team had seen off the Belgians 3-0 – he went home and said to his wife Nessie, "Tonight when I went out onto Anfield, there was a glow like a fire was burning."

That fire became very hard to extinguish over the next two decades. The 1970s saw Umbro make the kit which sported a white-trimmed round neck. That changed back to a V-neck in time for the club to become European Champions in 1977 and, in 1979, the club became the first in Britain to house a sponsor when Japanese electronics firm Hitachi paid to be associated with the now world famous red. Liverpool also adopted a distinctive yellow away jersey that year.

In 1982 came a change in style with a white pin-striped shirt and a white stripe down the shorts and Crown Paints now the kit sponsor. Adidas took responsibility for the shirt in

In 2006, more subtle methods of rebranding the shirt were employed

1985, with their three stripes on the shoulder alongside the familiar V-neck.

The 1987/88 kit had a rounder neck, while the following year Candy replaced Crown Paints as club sponsor. The most distinct development of that period was the grey away shirts followed by the speckled home kit of the 1989/90 championship winning team. It was, for many supporters, an acquired taste!

Into the 1990s and kits took on many different changes in order to satiate the marketing men – stripes on the shoulders, stripes on the ribs, a Reebok inspired return to the 1960s round neck.

A new century has seen turquoise kits, white kits, black and gold kits; for 2010/11 there is another new strip and new sponsor, Standard Chartered.

Colours and sponsors come and go but what remains is that fantasy. That wonderful thought that every match day when you put on your colours, you are actually one of the lucky ones to pull on the red jersey and play for the team.

The 2010/11 home kit, as close to classic as the modern age allows

HALL OF FAME

JOHN BARNES

For the hordes of Liverpool fans who enjoyed watching John Barnes terrorise opposing defences in the name of their football club in the late 1980s and 90s, regret is the furthest emotion from their minds.

Their number ten back then was arguably the best in the world but there must be some disappointment that his talent was never unleashed upon European opposition due to the ban on English clubs that followed the Heysal disaster of 1985.

Such were the heights that his game reached between 1987 and 1991 it would have whetted the appetite of every Koppite to see Barnes at his free-flowing best on a European night. AC Milan were the dominant force in those years and theirs was a special team housing the Dutch trio of Frank Rijkaard, Ruud Gullit and Marco Van Bastan, but would even they have had an answer to Barnes and his own special team-mates?

We will never know but you can be sure the usually

unflappable Franco Baresi and Paulo Maldini would have come off from any encounter looking troubled. Barnes was that good and it is a source of further regret that Bill Shankly never saw him pull on a red shirt, as he would have had the Scot drooling.

> **" Players like John Barnes come along just once in a lifetime "**
> Sir Tom Finney

Shankly loved a flying winger. He had adored Tom Finney and later brought both Peter Thompson and Steve Heighway to Liverpool's left flank with great success. The sight of Barnes skinning a couple of players before unleashing an unerring shot or wicked cross would have excited him as much as it did the fans.

Barnes was a linchpin in Kenny Dalglish's successful sides, winning player of the year on two occasions before an Achilles injury hampered his explosive power. In the 1990 title-winning season he scored an astonishing 22 goals while playing as a left winger – outscoring striker Ian Rush by four goals.

Like all greats he re-invented himself, becoming a tidy and wonderfully composed central midfielder in Roy Evans's attractive sides of the mid-nineties, this after making a public commitment to help develop young talent at the club.

Barnes left Liverpool in 1997 but the memories he gave so many will never disappear. Just a shame he never got at AC Milan!

Born: Kingston, Jamaica; 7th November 1963

Liverpool appearances: 409

Liverpool goals: 108

Honours won with Liverpool: First Division Championship (1987/88, 1989/90) FA Cup (1988/89, 1991/92), League Cup (1994/95)

Other clubs: Watford (1981-87), Newcastle (1997-99), Charlton (1999)

International appearances: England, 79

JOHN BARNES FACTFILE

IAN CALLAGHAN

As red flags swayed in the spring Rome night, Liverpool's back-room staff embraced. Bob Paisley, Joe Fagan and Rueben Bennett had all been around when Liverpool FC first took on European competition back in September 1964 under Bill Shankly.

Now, in 1977, they were European Champions and out on the pitch was a player who had shared in that incredible journey; Ian Callaghan.

As a quick, cerebral, crafty right-winger, Callaghan had starred in Shankly's first great team. In 1960, he'd dealt with the burden of replacing the illustrious Billy Liddell (not an easy task for a young man who grew up hero-worshiping the Scot) and it became clear Liverpool had a player of genuine quality.

After his debut – a 4-0 win over Bristol Rovers at Anfield – he was given a standing ovation by the 27,000 fans present, both sets of players and the referee! He was still winning plaudits 855 games later, his consistency and team-ethic never waned.

Callaghan, along with Peter Thompson on the opposite wing, gave Shankly's team of the 1960s its effervescence from wide areas. Roger Hunt and Ian St John fed on his crosses (St John's winner in the 1965 FA Cup final came from a typically elusive run and tempting cross from Callaghan) and his skills earned him a place in Alf Ramsey's victorious 1966 World Cup winning squad.

In 1970 Callaghan underwent knee surgery that many thought would end his Liverpool career (Kevin Keegan was bought as a possible replacement) but he simply reinvented himself as a central midfielder, where his workrate and ability to keep possession was pivotal in the club's success and its quest for the European Cup.

In 1978, Callaghan left for Swansea but did so having played more games than any other Red, a record that still holds today. Each of those 856 matches was played with a spirit and a genuine love for the club he so proudly represented.

> ❝ Ian Callaghan is everything good that a man can be. No praise is too high for him ❞
> Bill Shankly

Born: Toxteth, Liverpool; 10th April 1942

Liverpool appearances: 856

Liverpool goals: 68

Honours won with Liverpool:
First Division Championship (1963/64, 1965/66, 1972/73, 1975/76, 1976/77), Second Division Championship (1961/62), FA Cup (1964/65, 1973/74), European Cup (1976/77), UEFA Cup (1972/73, 1975/76)

Other clubs: Swansea City (1979-81), Crewe (1981-82)

International appearances: England, 4

IAN CALLAGHAN FACTFILE

KENNY DALGLISH

In the summer of 1966, a 15-year-old schoolboy trialist from Glasgow stood at the door of the first team dressing-room at Melwood, crippled by shyness but desperate to go in and get autographs from those men just crowned the new champions of England.

His fellow Scots Ian St John, Ron Yeats and Willie Stevenson were laughing behind the door but it took an age for the boy to open it.

Eventually he got his signatures but it was that timidity that perhaps saw him leave the club and return to his home town. Those players who he had pestered for autographs will have forgotten his baby face but 11 years later he returned and went on to become simply the greatest player the club has ever seen.

By 1977, Kenny Dalglish had already reached legendary status at Celtic but he craved European success. Liverpool, newly-crowned European Champions, had lost Kevin Keegan and so it was a match made in heaven, both parties giving the other all they had ever wanted.

The true greats of football share a hunger and desire for winning games. Pele, Diego Maradona, Zinedine Zidane; these men had all the skill but they also possessed a steely nature, a streetwise knowledge of how to compete. To that list of legends you can add Dalglish.

After games, the Scot's ankles would be bruised and lacerated by determined defenders' efforts but those same defenders would be nursing their own wounds, mostly inflicted upon their pride.

Dalglish was a master at shielding the ball, playing in his team-mates, opening up defences in a flash, and blockbuster shooting with either foot. As a player he brought trophies in abundance but more importantly, every week he made men and women of all ages happy to be in his presence and proud to support the team he so brilliantly gave everything for.

He didn't stop there. As manager he continued to bring in the silverware but more importantly looked after a public so devastated by the Hillsborough disaster of 1989. There have been so many greats at Liverpool FC but none were greater than him.

> **ff I just hoped that after the trials and tribulations of my early years in management, someone up high would smile on me and guide my hand. My plea was answered when we got Kenny Dalglish. What a player JJ**
> Bob Paisley

Born: Glasgow; 4th March 1951
Liverpool appearances: 515
Liverpool goals: 172
Honours won with Liverpool:
First Division Championship (1978/79, 1979/80, 1981/82, 1982/83, 1983/84, [as player/manager] 1985/86, 1987/88, 1989/90, FA Cup [as player/manager] (1985/86, 1988/89) League Cup (1980/81, 1981/82, 1982/83, 1983/84), European Cup (1977/78, 1980/81, 1983/84)
Other clubs: Celtic (1969-77)
International appearances: Scotland, 102

KENNY DALGLISH FACTFILE

ROBBIE FOWLER

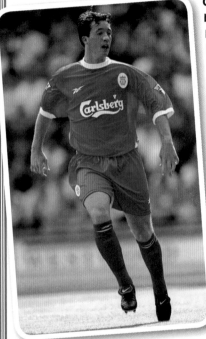

On a cold September night by the River Thames, Liverpool took on Fulham in the League Cup.

Only the most ardent fan would have been aware of a young striker who had been banging goals in for the reserves and who was getting his first start that night. A 3-1 win for the Reds wasn't the biggest news, but the goal scored by the 18-year-old Robbie Fowler sparked the start of a hero-worship from the terraces that would soon reach biblical proportions.

"God" – as Fowler would be known – scored all five in the second leg at Anfield and with the press banging on the dressing-room door, the manager simply told them that he wouldn't be talking to them as he wouldn't know what to say.

He may have been a callow and shy school kid off the pitch but Fowler was proving a deadly and self-assured striker on it. Manager Graeme Souness was sacked in

1994 but under Roy Evans, Fowler, along with many other fine young players, revamped the club's fortunes.

> ** I saw a lot of the young me in Robbie **
>
> Ian Rush

Fowler gave the club and its supporters goals, loads of goals. For three consecutive seasons up to 1997 he racked up more than 30 of them. A hat-trick in under four minutes against Arsenal, a double at Old Trafford that upstaged Eric Cantona's return from suspension, a screamer at Anfield against Villa. The list could go on but there was more to Fowler's appeal than the ball bulging the net. Liverpool fans adored Fowler because he was one of them.

With football and its protagonists becoming more and more withdrawn from the supporters, Fowler offered real edge. Whether it was the t-shirt he unveiled in support of the striking dockers or later, when he was at Manchester City, the four fingers he showed to Manchester United fans (as testament to the amount of European Cups then won by Liverpool), Fowler proved he was as cheeky and streetwise as any of those watching from the stands.

When he returned in 2006 after stints away, he was not the goalscorer he'd once been but he still had that spark and you get the feeling he always will.

Born: **Toxteth**; 9th April 1975
Liverpool Appearances: **369**
Liverpool goals: **183**
Honours won with Liverpool:
FA Cup (2000/01), League Cup (1994/95, 2000/01) UEFA Cup (2000/01)
Other clubs: Leeds United (2001-03), Manchester City (2003-06), Cardiff (2007-08), Blackburn (2008), North Queensland Fury (2009-)
International appearances: England, 26

ROBBIE FOWLER FACTFILE

STEVEN GERRARD

The Kop has two songs for Steven Gerrard. One celebrates how far he can pass the ball and just how hard he is, the other hails his captaincy and the fact that he is a Scouser born and bred.

The problem is, if they were to sing about every quality that he possesses they'd be looking at a songbook bigger than Lennon and McCartney's.

They would have to sing about every blade of grass he covers, about the unerring desire he has to win honours for the team he grew up adoring and about every brilliant goal he has managed when it mattered most.

You know a player is special when he is criticised for doing "too much", and while Gerrard has matured into a more refined version of his young swashbuckling self, you can't fault the man for his sheer bloody-minded will to win.

When he broke onto the scene, a fresh-faced but eager young man with the same crew cut and steely glare he still possesses today, everyone could see he was something special.

At worst it looked like Liverpool may have found their best ever right back (his early position), instead – as he matured and moved into midfield and later as a supporting striker of deadly quality – it has become clear to fans that they have been witnessing one of the club's and the game's all-time greats.

They say he has everything and they may have a point. His strikes from distance against Manchester United, Olympiakos and West Ham point to his brutal power, his clip over Shay Given at Newcastle in 2008 his deft touch, his partnership with Torres his eye for a team-mate.

His unforgettable display in the 2005 Champions League final where he went from the driving force to a tireless right back underlines his team ethic. He takes penalties and he can head the ball (just ask AC Milan). He tackles like the best of them and anyone who saw him pacify his giddy troops at Old Trafford after they went 3-1 up in February 2009 will tell you he is now not only a whole-hearted leader but a measured one too.

Two songs? It's not nearly enough!

> ** He is a player that I would like to have in my team **
> Kaka

Born: Whiston, Merseyside; 30th May 1980
Liverpool appearances: 532
Liverpool goals: 132
Honours won with Liverpool:
FA Cup (2000/01, 2005/06),
League Cup (2000/01, 2002/03),
European Cup (2004/05), UEFA Cup (2000/01)
Other clubs: none
International appearances: England, 80

STEVEN GERRARD FACTFILE

KEVIN KEEGAN

After 120 minutes of a gruelling FA Cup final in 1971, Liverpool's players trudged off the Wembley turf with their loser's medals after being beaten by double-winning Arsenal.

In the stands the despondent but proud fans were joined by a new signing snapped up by Bill Shankly just days before, a player who would go on to become a footballing megastar and one of the most important acquisitions in the club's history.

Bill Shankly had been badgered to look at Kevin Keegan for some time and, though impressed by the Scunthorpe midfielder, saw him as one for the future, so much so that he wasn't on the 1971/72 pre-season tour. However, in a practice match at Melwood just days before the new season, Keegan caused such mayhem that Shankly decided to give him his chance.

Twelve minutes into that first match at home to Nottingham Forest, Keegan pounced on a loose ball, put it into the Kop goal and never looked back. In his six seasons at the club, Keegan never played a reserve game.

The £35,000 that Shankly spent on Keegan were among the best spent by the club and it was the little striker's enthusiasm and sheer will to win that carried the club from being among the best to being the best.

The player they dubbed Mighty Mouse won the Championship and the UEFA Cup in his second season, the FA Cup in his third before – under Bob Paisley – winning two more titles, another UEFA Cup and in his last ever match for Liverpool, the European Cup in 1977.

Some Reds found it hard to fathom why Keegan would want to leave. But Keegan was quick to embrace the new football where endorsements and foreign money could be gained. The England captain went on to win the European Footballer of the Year award twice while at Hamburg, becoming a global star along the way.

What Liverpool fans will fondly recall though is Keegan not as superstar but as the diminutive footballer who worked as hard as he could to help himself and their club.

ff His performance proved that he's worth every Mark the Germans are paying for him ff
Bob Paisley after the 1977 European Cup final, Keegan's last game for the club

Born: Armthorpe, Doncaster; 14th February 1951

Liverpool appearances: 323

Liverpool goals: 100

Honours won with Liverpool: First Division Championship (1972/73, 1975/76, 1976/77), FA Cup 1973/74, European Cup (1976/77), UEFA Cup (1972/73, 1975/76)

Other clubs: Scunthorpe (1968-71), Hamburg (1977-80), Southampton (1980-82), Newcastle (1982-84)

International appearances: England, 63

KEVIN KEEGAN FACTFILE

BILLY LIDDELL

In 1968 Matt Busby was made a Knight of the Realm for some other work he did at some other club, but Liverpool fans would have gladly bestowed that same distinction upon him many years earlier, and all in honour of one short conversation.

As skipper of Liverpool in the 1930s, Busby went to his manager George Kay and said he had seen a gifted 16-year-old boy back in Scotland who was worth further inspection. That boy was Billy Liddell and once Kay had cast his eye over his talent, he was on his way to Liverpool and a celebrated career.

Liddell's guile, work ethic, shuddering power and gentlemanly persona endured him to his fans over 22 years in which his popularity became – at times – greater than that of the club. "Liddell-Pool" was the tag given to his side as he bolstered faltering morale in the lean years of the 1950s, having burst onto the scene in the championship winning side of 1946/47.

Having served in the RAF during the war, Liddell was demobbed just a few weeks into that first season after the hostilities and gave George Kay's team the ideal supply line for their eager centre-forwards. Jack Balmer and then Albert Stubbins thrived on Liddell's service and the 84 league goals scored by the victorious Reds were largely down to the blistering pace and accuracy of the Scot's wing-play.

His form showed no sign of decline for the following 15 years. While the club's fortunes dropped and relegation followed, it was Liddell, from either the wing or at centre forward, who kept the crowds coming.

Throughout his time there, Liddell managed to hold down his accountancy 'nine to five' job and along with Stanley Matthews is the only man to play for the Great Britain representative side on two occasions.

Liddell bowed out in August 1960 and every member of the Notts County team waited to shake his hand in the centre-circle on the final whistle. They, like the thousands of fans who adored him, were saying goodbye to a legend.

> **ff In my opinion, Liddell, Keegan and Dalglish were the club's best players ever, but I would put Billy ahead of the other two as being the greatest JJ**
> Ian Callaghan

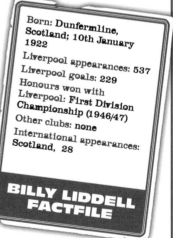

Born: Dunfermline, Scotland; 10th January 1922

Liverpool appearances: 537
Liverpool goals: 229
Honours won with Liverpool: First Division Championship (1946/47)
Other clubs: none
International appearances: Scotland, 28

BILLY LIDDELL FACTFILE

ALEX RAISBECK

Cutting a dashing figure with his head of blonde locks, tidy moustache and pristine red shirt, Alex Raisbeck was Liverpool's first superstar.

A fine centre half and skipper of the club's inaugural Championship-winning team, Raisbeck attracted attention from many an admirer, especially from those in the press. "A man of Raisbeck's proportions, style and carriage would rivet attention anywhere. He is a fine and beautifully balanced figure," gushed one scribe.

There was far more to the powerful Scot then mere aesthetics. Having impressed for Hibernian, Raisbeck joined Stoke in 1898 but didn't settle in the Potteries and so quickly went home.

On hearing of his countryman's exit, Liverpool director John McKenna sent manager Tom Watson north of the border on an express train with explicit instructions: Don't come back without Alex Raisbeck.

Watson didn't disappoint and immediately it was clear that the £350 they had spent on their new acquisition was incredibly shrewd. At just 5ft 10in, he was by no means a giant of a defender but he possessed such athleticism that bigger forwards were consistently beaten in aerial battles, whilst his superb tackling was the talk of the league. The 20-year-old commanded respect and Watson had no hesitation in making him skipper.

In 1901, Raisbeck became the first Liverpool man to lift the League Championship trophy. It was the same year in which the maximum wage was introduced and whilst players could not be paid more than £4 a week, the club guaranteed keeping their man by offering him additional work as a "bill inspector".

With his duties defined, Raisbeck continued to play at his swashbuckling best and, despite relegation, he led the team to successive promotion and championship winning seasons between 1905 and 1906.

The fans took to him as one of their own, especially as he showed such passion in the games against Everton. In 1909 they bid farewell to their first great idol but he would return 30 years later as chief scout, a position he kept until his death in March 1949.

> **ff He not only put body and dash into individual games he played, but more importantly he helped to create the soul, that inward sacred fire of zeal without which no club can thrive and live JJ**
> Victor Hall, *Liverpool Echo*

Born: Polmont, Scotland; 26th December 1878

Liverpool appearances: 340

Liverpool goals: 21

Honours won with Liverpool: First Division Championship (1900/01, 1905/06), Second Division Championship (1904/05)

Other clubs: Hibernian (1896-98), Stoke City (1898), Partick Thistle (1909-14), Hamilton Academicals (1914)

International appearances: Scotland, 8

ALEX RAISBECK FACTFILE

IAN RUSH

Ian Rush was by no means a flash footballer. When he scored (and he scored a lot) a finger pointed to the crowd and a smile to his team-mates was the best the television cameras could hope for.

To Rush, the act of putting a ball in a net was so natural that it deserved no histrionics. "The smile was one of contentment because I was continuing to do the job I was paid to do and loved to do – scoring goals," he said.

Not that goals always came so easy. After his arrival in April 1980, the young Rush struggled to find the net, and was told by Bob Paisley that his time at Liverpool would be a short one if he remained in awe of his surroundings and didn't get selfish.

A glut of goals followed and Paisley got the striker he always thought he had.

Rush's eye for goal became a sensation, with his manager's advice ringing in his ears his game – whilst seamlessly fitting into the club's team ethic – revolved around goals. With Dalglish alongside him and Graeme Souness behind, he was among greats but with each goal his icy temperament brought him he was playing himself into similar lofty echelons.

> **❝ We were made for each other ❞**
> Kenny Dalglish

Young Player of the Year in 1983, Player of the Year in 1984, his goals and the trophies they brought the club attracted attention from rich Italian clubs and, having smashed in the goals that won Liverpool the double in 1986, he signed for Juventus for £3.2m.

Fans campaigned for him to stay but their efforts fell on deaf ears. However, Kenny Dalglish re-signed him in 1988 and with his all-round game improved he set about breaking Roger Hunt's goalscoring records for the club before leaving again in 1996.

Today you'll find Rushie in the stands supporting the club and whenever a new striker comes along with goals in him, he will be compared to the man who simply scored more than any other.

Born: St Asaph, Wales; 20th October 1961

Liverpool appearances: 660
Liverpool goals: 346

Honours won with Liverpool:
First Division Championship (1981/82, 1982/83, 1983/84, 1985/86, 1989/90), FA Cup (1985/86, 1988/89), League Cup (1980/81, 1981/82, 1982/83, 1983/84, 1994/95), European Cup (1983/84)

Other clubs: Chester (1978-80), Juventus (1987-88), Leeds (1996-97), Newcastle (1997-98), Sydney Olympic (1998-2000)

International appearances: Wales, 73

IAN RUSH FACTFILE

ELISHA SCOTT

"Lisha, Lisha!" So cried a heaving Kop each time their iconic goalkeeper Elisha Scott ran out at Anfield.

With his trademark long-johns and protective knee-pads you could see the Ulsterman coming, and with his, shall we say, industrial Belfast language, team-mates, fans and the opposition could hear him too.

Having arrived at Liverpool in 1912, Scott played 467 times for the club (a record not broken until Billy Liddell managed it in the late 1950s), winning two championships and becoming one of the most recognisable footballing talents in the country.

A fearless competitor, Scott actually arrived at Anfield as a young man unsure that he had a future at the club. Recommended to manager Tom Watson by his big brother Bill, who had just left Everton where he was goalkeeper, Scott was initially seen as cover for Kenny Campbell.

Given his first game in January 1913 at Newcastle, Scott

immediately impressed and on the whistle of a goalless draw, the Newcastle board offered their Liverpool counterparts £1,000 for the 'reserve' keeper.

Scott himself suggested that Liverpool would be wise to accept it as he felt Campbell was such a good keeper that his own chances of first team action were going to be sparse. Watson had other ideas and a year later Scott was very much the club's custodian.

War curtailed much of his early promise but by the early 1920s Scott was a hugely popular character. "He is a great football personality with the eye of an eagle, the swift movement of a panther when flinging himself at shots and the clutch of a vice when gripping the ball," wrote one reporter.

On such a formidable base was Liverpool's successful team of the early 1920s built and back-to-back league titles were enjoyed between 1922 and 1923. Scott remained the club's most popular star until the early 1930s. A fan protest stopped a proposed move to Everton and in 1934 he played his last game for the club at Chelsea. He bowed out with an emotional speech at Anfield on the final day of that season.

> ❝ Elisha was the greatest I've ever seen. You can have Swift, Trautmann, Banks, Wilson. You can have them all. I'll take Elisha Scott ❞
>
> Everton's Dixie Dean

Born: Belfast; 24th August, 1894

Liverpool appearances: 467

Liverpool goals: 0

Honours won with Liverpool: First Division Championship (1921/22, 1922/23)

Other clubs: Linfield (1911), Broadway United (1911-12), Belfast United (1917-19 and 1934-36)

International appearances: Ireland, 31

ELISHA SCOTT FACTFILE

HILLSBOROUGH

> "It's 20 years on and it hasn't gone away, people still haven't been recompensed. It's still there, that black hole…"
>
> Roger McGough, Liverpudlian poet

There are those within the footballing fraternity who, 20 years after the nation's worst sporting disaster, believe that by now time should have healed. Whilst the majority of them are more than sympathetic to the plight of those who lost loved ones and were touched by the events at the Hillsborough Stadium on 15th April 1989, their advice is to "move on". Fellow fans, pundits, journalists – there are plenty who think it is time to forgive and forget.

If any of them had been present at Anfield on 15th April 2009, when 35,000 came to commemorate the 20th anniversary of the disaster, they would have left with a different opinion; for on that afternoon those present proved that this is by no means the time to forgive, to forget or to move on.

The Kop and Anfield pitch became a shrine in the days after the tragic events

Twenty years on and Anfield encapsulated every emotion that was so raw in the aftermath of the disaster and underlined that here is an issue that isn't just going to go away. There was grief; that will never disperse. There was anger, anger with an establishment that has chosen to leave too many political and judicial stones unturned, and – just as there was in April 1989 – there was a togetherness that transcends sport and evoked memories of the aftermath when Anfield became a place of communal prayer, remembrance and counselling.

Anfield's permanent memorial bears the names of those who lost their lives

It was a gloriously sunny day on 15th April 1989. Plans had been made for countless journeys from Liverpool to Sheffield in what was shaping up to be a glorious run-in for fans of the club. Match day butterflies and excitement would have been the travel companion of each fan making the trip across the Pennines.

Instead that day, the M62 that links the two cities witnessed a series of emotions that shouldn't be associated with football. That excitement in the morning was followed a few awful hours later by relatives rushing to Sheffield terrified of what awaited them, whilst the journey home for those whose fears had been realised was far, far worse.

Families could only watch at home while news bulletins

reached them. What should have been a memorable semi-final against Brian Clough's Nottingham Forest was turning into a nightmare, and in the end 96 supporters lost their lives after a crush in the Leppings Lane terrace at Sheffield Wednesday's stadium.

Having been faced with a large crowd outside the ground, the police ordered the opening of a gate, but rather than also opening the pens adjacent to the one immediately behind the goal, the fans were all ushered into the one pen. Within six minutes of the semi-final kicking off, it became clear that something was very wrong.

After 20 years, the search for answers and for justice goes on

In the absence of ambulances and medical help (only one ambulance was allowed near the pitch) fans began to use advertising hoardings to help ferry the injured to possible safety. Fans in the seating area above reached down to pull many from the terrace. Meanwhile the players and their manager sat nervously in the dressing-room relying on the drip, drip of information.

For years leading up to Hillsborough, football fans had been classed as second class citizens. The Heysal disaster was understandably still very fresh in people's minds and so it came as no surprise to fans that they would be the target of some scepticism. None of them, though, were ready for what happened days after the tragedy when *The*

Sun newspaper published what it termed "The Truth", in fact a series of lies about Liverpool fans at Hillsborough.

Such scurrilous efforts did not deter those who rallied around the bereaved. Liverpool Football Club had a player in attendance at every funeral (Kenny Dalglish and his wife Marina attended four in one day) and they kept vigils by the side of those injured or in comas.

The question of football resuming was inconsequential but the club and the players eventually felt the best way to honour those who died watching them play was to get on with playing. The FA Cup was won against Everton on an emotional day at Wembley while the league title was snatched in the last minute of the season by Arsenal.

The years after the Hillsborough disaster have seen football flourish commercially. There are those who feel it was that dramatic win for Arsenal at Anfield that helped save it from the doldrums. Others point to the 1990 World Cup. Football, though, didn't need saving. Those who have always loved it knew it would survive. The people that needed help were those who said goodbye to their loved ones expecting them to come home with tales of a football match. They didn't and those relatives are still looking for answers and for justice. They are the ones who need help and that is why those who advise that they "move on" are so wrong.

Steven Gerrard and Jamie Carragher display a certificate giving the victims' families freedom of the city at the memorial event

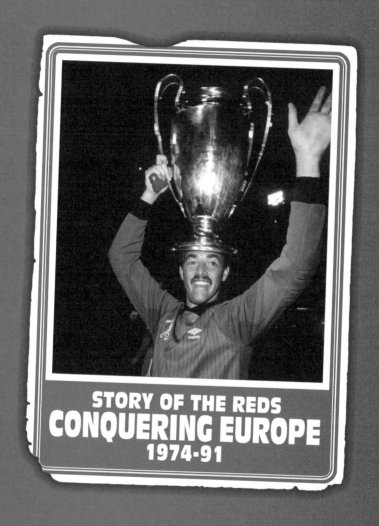

STORY OF THE REDS
CONQUERING EUROPE
1974-91

> "This club has been my life.
> I'd go out and sweep the
> street and be proud to do
> it for Liverpool FC if they
> asked me to"
>
> Bob Paisley

Everyone was in shock. Everyone. No one
had seen it coming. Fans looked crestfallen as stunned
television crews asked for their thoughts. There were
none. Just stunned silence. Bill Shankly himself told his
subjects that he had for too long ignored his family and
now was the right time to be with them.

It was a decision that the great man would later freely
admit that he regretted but for now the club's board
had the unenviable task of finding a man to fill
Shankly's considerable boots. Outsiders were
considered but none seemed to fit. The answer it
seemed lay closer to home with a man who knew
Shankly's ways best, his assistant Bob Paisley.

Bob Paisley was the archetypal reluctant hero.
His aversion to commit to the job was born of a
knowledge that whoever took over from Shankly
would be hampered by the glorious shadow cast over
the place by his achievements and personality. Those
fears were realised in his first season and in late 1974
things had got very tough for team and manager alike.

Seemingly out of the title race, out of the cup and out of Europe, members of the press smelt blood and began questioning Paisley's know how. Soon though the quiet Paisley began to bed in and even enjoy his role.

His debut season finished without a trophy but Paisley had started to shape his team. The full back Phil Neal was signed, Terry McDermott came in and Ray Kennedy (Shankly's last ever signing) was converted from striker to playmaking midfielder.

The title found its way home for a record ninth time in 1975/76 and was once more joined by the UEFA Cup. Paisley had proved the doubters wrong. He was aware that even success would have some claiming that it was "Shankly's team", but this was Paisley's side working and gelling under his modest but expert tuition.

The 1976/77 season saw yet another championship won, but even better was the European run that

Captain Emlyn Hughes lifts the European Cup in Rome after Liverpool's 1977 victory over Borussia Monchengladbach

THE POCKET BOOK OF LIVERPOOL

This time it's Paris, 1981 as Alan Kennedy and Phil Neal celebrate beating Real Madrid

reached the heights in March with a famous 3-1 win over St Etienne and finished with the glory of Rome and a 3-1 victory over Borussia Monchengladbach.

The team got better and better. When Kevin Keegan left, the club recruited Kenny Dalglish and simply improved things. Dalglish, Graeme Souness, Alan Hansen, they all came in after that 1977 European Cup victory and went onto take the trophy three times for themselves. Paisley himself became the only manager to win the famous trophy three times after victories in 1978 and 1981 against Bruges and Real Madrid respectively.

Despite trophies cascading into Anfield and a new team inspired by the goals of lethal marksman Ian Rush, Paisley retired in 1983. Seamless continuity reigned once more and this time Joe Fagan was promoted from within. His first season finished with a treble of the Championship, League Cup and European Cup.

Fagan's second and last season was more problematic. Souness had left for Italy and for the first time in a long time, Liverpool found quality hard to replace. The club had to settle for second place in the league.

Then, events before the European Cup final against Juventus at Heysal on 29th May, when 39 fans in the Italian section of the ground died trying to escape onrushing Liverpool supporters, left Fagan and the club under a dark cloud.

Fagan had declared his retirement prior to the game but hoped to come home a hero. Instead he landed at Liverpool airport in tears. It was no way for a legend to bow out.

Many were shocked by Kenny Dalglish's appointment as player-manager. Reeling from the disaster at Heysal, the club were open for criticism and there were those who felt the appointment was far from the Liverpool way. A gamble not becoming of Anfield's steady ship.

They looked right in February 1986 after a 2-0

defeat at home to Everton left them well off the pace of their local rivals. That night Dalglish took his friend and club captain Alan Hansen to dinner. There the centre half regrettably informed the boss that he thought this was the worst Liverpool side he'd ever played in. Dalglish took stock, picked himself for the remaining matches and incredibly led the side to their

Rome again in 1984, for a clash with Roma that the Reds would win on penalties

first ever League and FA Cup double. Beating Everton
to both trophies was merely a bonus.

It was an incredible first season. The Danish
midfielder Jan Molby blossomed under the Scot, Gary
Gillespie came in impressively, the unsung Kevin
Macdonald was a revelation in the middle and Ian

Rush just didn't stop scoring.

Those goals attracted Juventus's Lira and so, with the marksman gone, Dalglish set about forming a new, even better team. Former Koppite John Aldridge came in for the Welshman, Peter Beardsley arrived to fill Dalglish's number seven jersey and John Barnes zigzagged his way into the fans' hearts with some quite electrifying displays.

The team that won the title in 1987/88 was arguably the club's best, but a shock defeat at Wembley against Wimbledon cost them another double. The following season saw a double once more snatched from under the club's nose. The FA Cup was won against Everton but Arsenal took the league with a dramatic last minute winner at Anfield.

But the season was overshadowed by the events of 15th April 1989 when 96 Liverpool fans died simply supporting the side they loved in the FA Cup semi-final at Hillsborough.

It was an event that visibly shook Dalglish and although he steered the club to an 18th Championship in 1990, the pressure had taken its toll and, in February 1991, he stepped down from a job and a club he so clearly loved.

Ian Rush peels away, arm aloft, after scoring his first, Liverpool's second, against Everton in an emotional 1989 FA Cup final

TACTICS

SHANKS GOES 4-4-2

There are those who will tell you that it was Alf Ramsey who came up with the 4-4-2 formation that won England the 1966 World Cup. People at Liverpool would beg to differ; or as Tommy Smith succinctly puts it, "That's a load of s***e! It was Shanks and Liverpool in 1964".

That year Liverpool had drawn Anderlecht in the European Cup. Shankly had seen the Belgian national side recently out-smart England and earn a 2-2 draw at Wembley. With much of the Anderlecht team in that side, the Scot realised he needed to do something clever to nullify their threat going forward.

The 19-year-old Tommy Smith was given the number 10 shirt, usually that worn by the inside forward playing the old WM formation used at the club. Instead, Smith was told by Shanks and his staff to get back and be a second centre half alongside Ron Yeats. "He wanted to shore up the defence and I would be Big Ron's right leg," recalls Smith. "Great player the big man, but no right foot." The game was won 3-0 and the formation stuck.

The outside right (Ian Callaghan) and outside left (Peter Thompson) became more orthodox wingers in a four man midfield and the inside right moved up front to make a two-man strikeforce. The back four would remain flat, encouraging the then goalkeeper Tommy Lawrence to act as a sweeper, a tradition later upheld by Ray Clemence and then Bruce Grobbelaar.

"It worked very well and we kept it going," says Smith. "That year we won the Cup and I think Ramsey must have had a look at our success and liked what he saw."

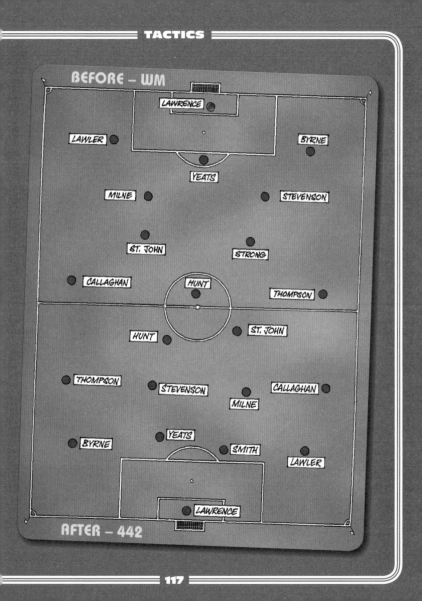

4-4-2 TO 4-5-1

In the mid-1980s Sammy Lee was asked by a journalist who he thought was the best defender at the club. "Alan Hansen? Mark Lawrenson?"

"Ian Rush", answered Lee. This might be a strange thing to say about a man who scored 346 goals for the club but Lee had a point and was alluding to the work Rush would do off the ball, a tactic that paid huge dividends away from home, especially in Europe.

In 1983/84 Liverpool won the European Cup the hard way. Three times they had tricky second-legs away from home and in the final they beat Roma in Rome. Liverpool played their basic 4-4-2 with Dalglish and Rush making a formidable strikeforce, but away in the most intimidating of stadiums the team could change seamlessly to a 4-5-1 with Dalglish perfect at slipping back into midfield to sure things up.

This hardly left the team toothless up front as Rush's work was so unselfish that he would prevent the opposition from starting attacks. "People don't realise how good Rushie was away from home," recalls Mark Lawrenson. "He was our first defender. He'd have the full backs not wanting the ball because he was onto them. He would look out of the corner of his eye, pretending not to be aware but as soon as the keeper moved his arm he was off haring after the defender." Opposing teams were harassed into losing possession and from there Liverpool could mount their attacks.

"It helped having Kenny in the hole," says Ian Rush. "He had the know-how to be the conduit of the team. He was the hub around which everything revolved."

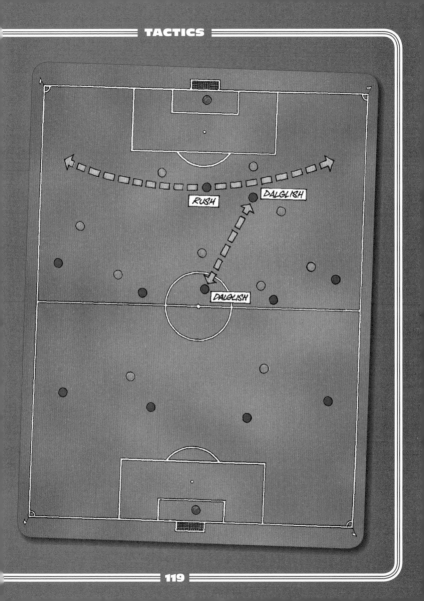

WING-BACKS AND MACCA

By 1995, Liverpool manager Roy Evans had started to build his team, a team that he hoped would take the club back to the pinnacle of the English game. That never quite happened but under the amiable Scouser the club played some of the most expansive and entertaining football around, with a crop of young players who put the club back on the map.

They would of course be labelled "The Spice Boys" for their supposed nocturnal habits but that does them a disservice. Under Evans and his 3-4-1-2 system Liverpool – especially during the 1995-96 season – played some scintillating football, beating all-comers including Manchester United, Newcastle (who will forget the 4-3 match at Anfield?) and Arsenal.

Evans had inherited an ageing squad in 1994 but with some emerging talent he had bags of potential to work with. He brought two new centre backs (Phil Babb and John Scales) to join Neil Ruddock or Mark Wright at the back, gave John Barnes a midfield berth where his range of passing and experience were best suited, and deployed wing-backs in Rob Jones and Jason McAteer, who were both experts at the more advanced roles their positions required.

The key to the formation though was in Steve McManaman's position. For many he was the heir apparent to Barnes on the wing but, by giving him a free role, Evans allowed the youngster to wreak havoc on opposing defences. He would drop deep, drift wide, pop up in attack and was the perfect foil for Stan Collymore and the emerging talent of Robbie Fowler.

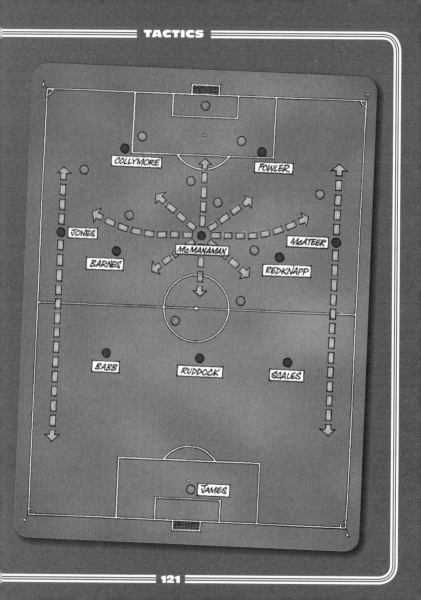

GERRARD AND TORRES IN 4-2-3-1

Under Rafa Benitez, Valencia played a 4-2-3-1 formation and won two La Liga titles plus the UEFA Cup. It took a few seasons for the Spaniard to implement the system at Anfield but once he got the personnel in place, it worked a treat, tempting some onlookers to label his team "Pool-encia".

"It is more or less the same system," admitted Bentez. In 2007 he signed Javier Mascherano, perfect in a two man deeper midfield. Xabi Alonso, far from merely a holding midfielder, gave the side balance and a fine range of passing while it was the three playing off the central striker that had to work, offering goals and – when possession was lost – cover in midfield.

Dirk Kuyt, a prolific striker while in Holland, was perfect on the right hand side of the three. He can score goals but his tireless efforts off the ball (Benitez called him 'Mr Duracell') nullified the most forward thinking of left backs.

In Spain, Benitez had the skills of the Argentine playmaker Pablo Aimar complimenting the more robust John Carew up front. At Liverpool he had Steven Gerrrad off Fernando Torres.

In the media many have put fingers to keypads to discuss Gerrard's best position but it is obvious that that advanced position off a central striker allows him the freedom to do his most destructive work and in Torres he had the perfect partner.

Torres is a deadly finisher but he also leads a line so well. He may not be as physically imposing as Carew but he has equal strength and can hold the ball up whilst also possessing the agility to spin and move on to through balls.

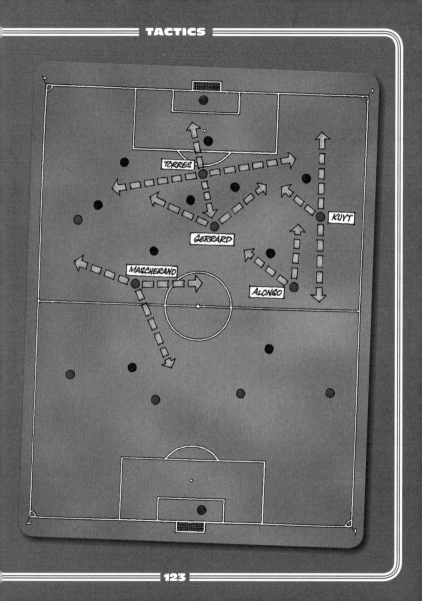

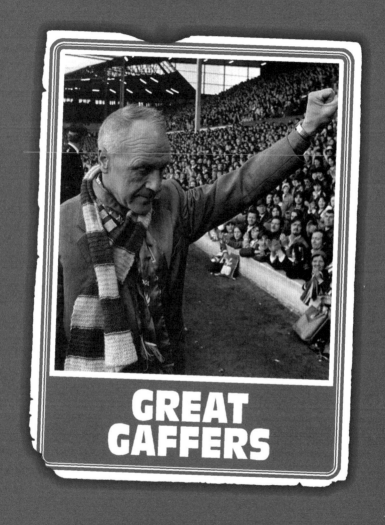

GREAT
GAFFERS

> "A manager who is honest with his players can transmit his thoughts to them. I'm certain I've headed a few in and I've kept some out too."

Bill Shankly

For almost 120 years, thousands upon thousands of men, women and children have flocked to Anfield to watch the match. Generation after generation has passed on a passion for the club and as success and fame has followed, millions more from every corner of the globe have seen fit to call Liverpool their team.

First manager John McKenna is honoured by a plaque at Anfield

In all those years, only 17 men have held the responsibility to shape and mould that team; only 17 men have had the honour of calling themselves 'Manager'.

In 1892, having overseen the split from Everton and housed his new club at Anfield, John Houlding's first appointments were William Barclay and John McKenna. Officially both were directors but in reality they were the club's first managers. Barclay would oversee administration, McKenna looked after the team.

McKenna had a way about him that screamed 'progress' and in 1896 he persuaded Tom Watson, the country's finest coach, to come to Anfield from Sunderland. Watson's Wearsiders had won three league titles in the 1890s and it was the amiable Geordie's sheer professionalism (Watson drew up a nutritional list that included the sparing use of sugar, potatoes and tobacco) that brought the first Championship to Liverpool in 1901.

Watson may have also presided over relegation but such was his passion and astute movement in the transfer market that, between 1909 and 1910, the club became the first to win promotion and the title in successive years. The club's first FA Cup final appearance followed in 1914, but a year later, having been in charge for 19 years (still a record for a Liverpool manager), Tom Watson died.

War meant that Liverpool didn't appoint another boss until 1920. A roaring decade was underway but in David Ashworth the club appointed a quiet man. His team though were his antithesis and in 1922 and 1923 won back-to-back titles. Not that the manager hung around for his second championship medal, strangely choosing to leave halfway through the season for bottom placed Oldham.

Bill Shankly revolutionised the club

From left: Joe Fagan, Roy Evans and Ronnie Moran with goalkeeper Bruce Grobbelaar in the Anfield bootroom

Matt McQueen and then George Patterson led Liverpool into the thirties but these were lean years and, in 1936, Patterson was replaced by George Kay, a hearty Mancunian who would remain at the helm until the early fifties.

The first post-war title was won in 1947 after Kay had advocated a tour of America, citing the need for his players (many who had come home from battle) to get a quota of sunshine, fresh orange juice and red meat before the season got under way.

Kay brought the title and a 1950 FA Cup final appearance (he also brought Bob Paisley!) but stress and illness saw him retire in 1951. Under his successors, Don Welsh and Phil Taylor, the club struggled. Both were good men but with the club sitting in the second division, good wasn't enough. What Liverpool needed was a hurricane. In December 1959 that hurricane arrived and blew them into the upper echelons of the world game.

Bill Shankly. The name still has an iconic hold on all football fans. The man revolutionised the club, bringing unprecedented success and set about doing what to him was most important, "Making the people happy".

Under Shankly, Liverpool won promotion, three League titles, two FA Cups and the UEFA Cup. Crowds flocked to Anfield and when, in 1974, he resigned the furore that followed was tantamount to the death of a monarch.

Who could replace the king? Far from a monarchist himself, Shankly had built a dynasty and so the answer lay within. Quiet, restrained, even reluctant, Bob Paisley took over and somehow managed to outdo even Shankly.

A glut of trophies followed, won both at home and abroad by a man with an incredible feel for both the game and its people. Paisley joked that a talented footballer should only ever utter three sentences. "Not my fault, I was tight on my man"; "I was in space, you should have passed to me" and, "That's a great idea, boss".

When Paisley stepped down in 1983 Joe Fagan, a stalwart of the legendary Liverpool boot-room, seamlessly took charge and in his first season in

Bob Paisley with the 1978 European Cup

1983/84, took an incredible treble of League, League Cup and European Cup.

After the tragedy of Heysal, Fagan was replaced by Kenny Dalglish. He was only 34, and the appointment was seen by critics as hasty. But the Scotsman won the double in his first season. Two more championships and another FA Cup followed.

More important was his handling of the Hillsborough disaster. Dalglish, along with his wife Marina, will long be remembered for their dedication to the victims and their families. Dalglish offered warmth and a presence that helped so many in need.

Player-manager Kenny Dalglish celebrates the 1990 league title with coaches Ronnie Moran and Roy Evans

It might have been the toll of those actions that saw Dalglish resign in 1991. What followed was a decade of – by Liverpool's standards – mediocrity. Graeme Souness stepped in (after Ronnie Moran had filled the roll of caretaker) but was never the same influence from the sidelines that he'd been in midfield.

In 1994, Liverpool went back to basics and the boot-room legacy was reborn. Roy Evans had retired young as a player but enjoyed success as reserve team manager. In the main job Evans produced an attractive team capable of success but one that would be remembered for its white Wembley suits and 'Spice Boy' tag.

It was unfair on Evans but in 1998 the board brought in Frenchman Gerard Houllier, first as his co-manager and, when that predictably failed, as his replacement. Houllier, as part of the French World Cup winning set-up, had the credentials and in Sami Hyypia and Dietmar Hamann brought the right type of player to the club.

In 2000/01 he guided the club to a treble of trophies. Illness and a poor record in the transfer market curtailed further success and in 2004 he was replaced by Rafael Benitez of Spain.

A success at Valencia, Benitez went to work but even he must have been flabbergasted when his first season ended with that glorious night in Istanbul. The FA Cup followed and the Premier League was seemingly a tangible reality but then, after a calamitous 2009/10 season, the Spaniard left.

Gerard Houllier with the 2001 UEFA Cup

Outsiders had berated some Liverpool fans for suporting Benitez through that hard period but the position of manager, if understood – as Benitez so clearly did – is sacrosanct and any man who follows in the footsteps of Shankly, Paisley, Fagan and Dalglish will never walk alone.

Rafa the gaffer achieved success in spite of difficult circumstances

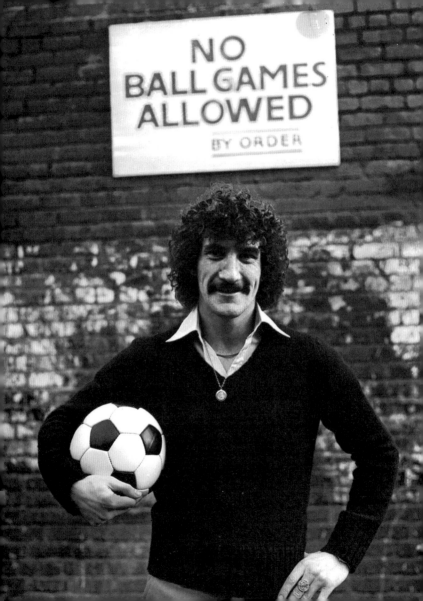

MEMORABLE MATCHES

LIVERPOOL 2 LEEDS UTD 1

FA Cup final, Wembley Stadium, 1st May 1965

Seventy-three years, 207 FA Cup ties, and two lost finals had passed under the bridge when Bill Shankly's Liverpool arrived at Wembley to once more try and win the FA Cup.

Leeds United hoped that, like Burnley and Arsenal before them, they could frustrate the Reds' big day but instead found that nothing, not even the damp North London weather, was going to ruin this scouse party.

Liverpool had overcome Chelsea in the semi-final and arrived confident that they could add to the league title win just 12 months earlier. The match itself was a cagey affair. Don Revie's young side were already known for their physicality and in just the third minute, Liverpool's left back Gerry Byrne clashed with Bobby Collins. Unbeknown to his team-mates he broke his collar bone but, with no substitutes, Byrne manfully played on and had a blinder as Liverpool began to get a grip on the soggy Wembley turf.

This was a resolute Leeds though and, with Gary Sprake in their goal making saves, Liverpool were frustrated. After 90 minutes there was no score, but this was a strong Liverpool team, trained harder than any other by a fitness fanatic manager who simply told his team that their opponents would soon wilt on the big pitch.

Just three minutes in to extra time, he was proved right. Byrne got to the bye-line and

Liverpool apply the pressure in the May Day final

swept in a cross which Roger Hunt headed home. Uncharacteristically Liverpool then immediately took their eye off the ball and allowed Billy Bremner to volley home.

Shankly will have been seething but the strength he had instilled into his team saw them keep the ascendancy and with just nine minutes left Ian St John stooped to head in the winner after great work from Ian Callaghan down the right wing.

The cup was won at last. The players took the plaudits as the biggest day in the English football calendar finally belonged to them. "We went up to get our medals," recalls Ian Callaghan. "I couldn't say anything to the Queen. I couldn't say anything to anyone." Words were unnecessary; actions were doing very nicely indeed.

Liverpool:
Lawrence, Lawler, Byrne, Strong, Yeats, Stevenson, Callaghan, Hunt, St John, Smith, Thompson

Scorers:
Hunt, St John

Attendance:
100,000

LIVERPOOL 3 BORUSSIA MOENCHENGLADBACH 1

European Cup final, Stadio Olimpico, Rome, 25th May 1977

How appropriate that it should be in the Eternal City of Rome that Liverpool Football Club would put on a performance that will forever be remembered by those who hold the club dear.

Twenty-three years after their first ever European match in icy Reykjavik, the club were finally crowned European Champions and, despite four further winning finals, for many this night in Italy will always be the special one.

When the club arrived they did so off the back of an FA Cup final defeat at Wembley just four days earlier but, having won the title, this was a confident bunch and in their manager they were in the hands of a master. Bob Paisley joked that the last

Terry McDermott beats Bertie Vogts and goalie Wofgang Kneib to make it 1-0

time he was in Rome was in a tank in 1944 when he helped liberate the place!

With that relaxed frame of mind, Liverpool took to the field with a confident ease. They may have been playing a team packed full of West Germany's 1974 World Cup-winning squad but with Kevin Keegan working tirelessly in front of a combative midfield, it was they who early on looked the likely winners.

After the excitement of their quarter-final win over St Etienne, many of the fans who had got to Rome by hook or by crook believed they were destined to win it and, just 28 minutes in, they were in front after Terry McDermott finished off a slick move.

Moenchengladbach hit back in the second half with an equaliser that should have knocked the stuffing out of Paisley's men but, like their manager in 1944, they had an old tank to call on in Tommy Smith and it was the fully armoured Scouser who, with 25 minutes left, climbed high to head them back in front.

A late penalty won by the departing Kevin Keegan and converted by Phil Neal put the game beyond doubt and saw the club start a friendship with the old trophy that to this day is as close as ever. "This is the greatest night in the history of Liverpool Football Club," said a beaming Bob Paisley.

Liverpool:
Clemence, Neal, Jones, Smith, Kennedy, Hughes, Keegan, Case, Heighway, Callaghan, McDermott

Scorers:
McDermott, Smith, Neal (pen)

Attendance:
57,000

LIVERPOOL 5
NOTTINGHAM FOREST 0

First Division, Anfield, 13th April 1988

Bill Shankly would have been a proud man. Not only was the performance as majestic as possibly ever seen at Anfield but it was his old team-mate at Preston Tom Finney, a player he regarded as one of the greatest of all time, who declared it as maybe the best of all time.

"I think that's one of the finest exhibitions of football I've ever seen the whole time I've played and watched the game. You couldn't see it bettered anywhere – not even in Brazil. The moves they put together were fantastic," said Finney.

Even Des Waker couldn't stop John Aldridge

Nottingham Forest came to Anfield as one of the of the country's top teams but just couldn't live with a fine Liverpool side. The Reds had put on awesome displays all season, but unfortunately for Brian Clough's men, never quite at this extraordinary level.

Wave after brilliant wave of attack thrilled the crowd, who never knew where the next one might start. Alan Hansen would glide forward, John Barnes would dribble inside, Steve

Beardsley in particular was outstanding

McMahon would drive from deep or Peter Beardsley would appear from nowhere.

It was Hansen who elegantly stepped forward to feed the industrious Ray Houghton for their 18th minute lead and, after a wonderful pass from Beardsley, John Aldridge doubled that lead before half-time. Beardsley went on one run that took him past four defenders, only to rattle the crossbar and bring the whole crowd to its feet.

Forest possessed England defenders in Stuart Pearce and Des Walker but such was the invention they faced, the floodgates were always likely to burst.

Gary Gillespie banged in a third before the best goal of the night summed up the performance. Barnes took the ball to the left-hand corner flag and nutmegged Steve Chettle before pulling it back for Beardsley to fire home. Aldridge grabbed a fifth four minutes from time to put an end to a phenomenal display.

"That one night captured all that was great about our team," said John Barnes. "Movement, pace, flair, strength, it was all on show. I loved every minute of it."

Liverpool:
Grobbelaar, Gillespie, Ablett, Nicol, Spackman, Hansen, Beardsley, Aldridge, Houghton (Johnston), McMahon (Molby), Barnes

Scorers:
Houghton, Aldridge (2), Gillespie, Beardsley

Attendance:
39,535

LIVERPOOL 3 AC MILAN 3*
Champions League final, Ataturk Stadium, Istanbul, 26th May 2005

The best striker in Europe is putting the ball on the spot. He, like his team-mates, has the look of a beaten man but still, this is Andrei Shevchenko, a man who has made a career of unerringly sticking the ball into the net.

Should he miss though, Liverpool will be European Champions. European Champions! Just a crazy couple of hours earlier, the very thought that that might happen seemed bizarre at best.

From the first minute of the match when Paulo Maldini put Milan one-nil up, things had looked

ominous. But Liverpool actually had some good spells in the first half, only to be hit by two Hernan Crespo sucker punches.

As the players sat dejected in the dressing-room while their manager somehow found the serenity to talk tactics, they could hear the feint cries of *You'll Never Walk Alone* from their army of fans. "I'd like to say it inspired me," said Jamie Carragher. "If I'm honest though, it made me feel much worse. They're doing their bit and we haven't done ours".

After another tricky start though, those feelings of despair went from hope and on to sheer amazement as goals from Gerrard, Smicer and Alonso turned the game upside down. Milan's superstars kept coming but found a team whose cast-iron hearts outweighed their lead-like legs. Carragher flew at tackles, cramp as well as Shevchenko and Crespo his enemy; Gerrard played everywhere, and through the latter stages and extra-time, Dudek was a man possessed.

And so now, here we were, Shevchenko versus Dudek. The ball is on the spot, the referee blows his whistle and the Ukrainian is unconfidently approaching the ball. Right foot… Well you know the wonderful rest. In Istanbul we won it five times!

★ Liverpool won 3-2 on penalties

Liverpool:
Dudek, Finnan (Hamann), Carragher, Hyypia, Traore, Riise, Gerrard, Alonso, Garcia, Kewell (Smicer), Baros (Cisse)

Scorers:
Gerrard, Smicer, Alonso

Attendance:
65,000

**STORY OF THE REDS
NEW ADVENTURES
1991-2010**

> "It feels as if I have been on a permanent honeymoon since I arrived here, I am on a cloud and I feel as if with Liverpool I have found the love of my life"
>
> Rafa Benitez

The day after Kenny Dalglish stunned the world of football by resigning as the club's iconic manager, the team had to travel south for a match at Luton, in a league they remained top of and still hoped to win.

Boot-room stalwart Ronnie Moran was, as ever, on hand to take over the reins and as he looked at a dressing-room full of good but shell-shocked professionals, he tried to keep their minds on the job at hand.

"We'll all miss Kenny," he said. "These things happen in life and the only thing that matters now is beating Luton and going from there." That was the Liverpool way. Whether in glory or adversity, the club had always looked ahead but times were changing and things were no longer so straightforward.

That day, Liverpool lost 1-0, their form dipped and Arsenal won the title. Before the season was out though, the Liverpool board acted swiftly (some say

too swiftly, as Dalglish might have been tempted back) and replaced one legend with another.

Graeme Souness's arrival appeased many concerned fans. They had always hero-worshiped him and he had done a great job in his first managerial role at Rangers. At Liverpool though, it wasn't to be.

There were good moments. The return to Europe, the 1992 FA Cup win and Souness's faith in youngsters such as Steve McManaman and Robbie Fowler were highlights but, if anything, the manager tried too hard and made too many changes, too quickly.

A massive drop down the league table, FA Cup

Steve McManaman was one of the young stars who lifted the FA Cup in 1992

defeats at the hands of Bolton and then Bristol City (both at Anfield), and a very misguided exclusive in *The Sun* on the day of the third anniversary of the Hillsborough disaster meant that Souness took the club into the new Premier League era as the club's most unpopular manager in a generation and in 1994 he left the club he had so hoped to be successful at.

It was time to go back to basics and in Roy Evans

Liverpool had a man on the staff who was a symbol of a simpler time. But Evans wouldn't be sitting on that past. The likes of Ronnie Whelan, Bruce Grobbelaar, Jan Molby and Steve Nicol were legends but the new man recognised changes had to be made.

He would later be chastised for being "too nice", but Evans wasn't scared of ringing in those changes. Souness had left him a fine crop of youngsters and they'd become the energy on which his team was based.

With the Kop knocked down in the summer of 1994, Anfield's new look symbolised a new start and the new team impressed with their flowing football. By winning the 1995 League Cup, they proved that further success might not be far away.

That summer Stan Collymore, costing a club record £8.5 million, forged a crackling strike-force with Robbie Fowler. The young Scouser by now was on fire, scoring goal after goal. Here were new heroes but ultimately they would be classed as a team who came so close. Calling them "underachievers" might be cruel but with football and its protagonists becoming richer and richer the label of "Spice Boys" was inevitable.

Despite an FA Cup final in 1996 and challenging

The 2001 UEFA Cup win was part of an unprecedented cup treble

for the title in 1997, Evans's tenure was under threat and in the summer of 1998, when Gerard Houllier was asked to come in as a "co-manager", his days looked well and truly numbered. The project never took off and just days after a woeful exit from the League Cup at the hands of Spurs, Evans cut off a 33-year love affair with his local club.

Houllier was a student of the game; he had worked in the city in the seventies and seemed to get the club and its fans. In the summer of 1999 he bought Sami Hyypia and Dietmar Hamann, the following year he bought Gary McAllister, home grown talent such as Jamie Carragher and Steven Gerarrd had broken through and suddenly the Frenchman had a team gelling and likely to win things.

In fact – in 2000/01 – they won three things, a treble of trophies that while not including the holy grail of the Premier League, offered party after party for Reds fans everywhere. Birmingham were beaten at Cardiff in the League Cup final, the same venue hosted the FA Cup final in which a remarkable Michael Owen late show saw off Arsenal and, in the UEFA Cup, Alaves were beaten 5-4 in a breathtaking final in Dortmund.

Liverpool were back at the fore of the European game. A quarter-final place in the following season's

Champions League plus a runners–up spot in the Premier League suggested even better was to come but, once more, expectations weren't met.

Some questionable decisions in the transfer market put Houllier on the back foot and even a League Cup final win over United in 2003 couldn't keep the

Rafa the Gaffer became Senor Popular after winning trophies in each of his first two seasons

wolves from the door. Champions League football was guaranteed at the end of the 2003/04 season but it wasn't enough. Houllier left after six topsy-turvy seasons and in came a Spaniard who in his homeland had broken up the dominance of two major clubs to win major honours. It was hoped that Rafa Benitez could do the same in England.

Benitez knew he had a job on his hands – league defeats at Southampton and Birmingham confirmed those thoughts – but in the Champions League with his know-how and the team's ever-growing belief, the miracle of Istanbul got closer and closer.

Incredible European nights at home to Juventus and Chelsea were just a prelude to what happened in Turkey where the team came from 3-0 down to stun a quite brilliant AC Milan team and win on penalties.

Like a long lost old friend, the European Cup made its way back to Anfield (and as the club's fifth it's where it stays), a possible move away from his home by Steven Gerarrd was averted, the 2006 FA Cup was won (due largely to the skipper's efforts) and Benitez, in becoming the first Reds manager to win trophies in both his first two seasons, was Senor Popular!

Less popular have been Tom Hicks and George Gillett Jnr, the new American owners, who since their acquisition of the club in 2007 have failed to convince fans that their intentions are honourable.

Benitez brought Fernando Torres, a hero in the same mould as Messrs Dalglish, Rush and Fowler and by doing so built a team that came closer than any

A fifth European Cup was lifted after the Miracle of Istanbul in 2005

Reds' side in the Premiership era to winning the title. But things didn't go to plan and he was replaced in June 2010 by Roy Hodgson. Whatever happens next the fans, the real lifeblood of the club, will turn up to watch the team with hope in their hearts.

YOU'LL NEVER WALK ALONE

"When you walk through a storm
Hold your head up high
And don't be afraid of the dark

At the end of the storm
Is a golden sky
And the sweet silver song of the lark

Walk on through the wind
Walk on through the rain
Though your dreams be tossed and blown

Walk on walk on with hope in your heart
And you'll never walk alone
You'll never walk alone"

Any fan who stood on the Kop in its terraced heyday will tell you that it was a place a million miles away from the showbiz world of a Broadway or West End musical. The industrial language, the rasping wit and the manly smells were undeniably football but the song that became its anthem started out its life in the fluffier world of show-tunes.

You'll Never Walk Alone was written by the famous impresarios Richard Rogers and Oscar Hammerstein

YOU'LL NEVER WALK ALONE

for their 1945 musical *Carousel*. The song is sung three times during the show, including as the rousing crescendo and it is that uplifting nature that has seen the song become synonymous with the club.

The song had already been a massive post-war hit for the likes of Frank Sinatra (1945) and Nina Simone (1959) when Merseybeat band Gerry and the Pacemakers recorded it in 1963. Later that decade, both Pattie LaBelle (1964) and Elvis Presley (1968) enjoyed success with the song.

By the early 1960s the Kop, always full long before kick-off, had taken to singing and adapting current hits. The Routers' 1962 hit *Let's Go* was changed to "*One-two, One-two-three, One-two-three-four, St John*". A tune later used to honour Dalglish, Fowler and Torres.

As well as changing the words to songs the Kop would

It was Gerry and the Pacemakers' chart-topping hit in 1963 that inspired the Kop

always join in when that week's Number One was played on the ground's tannoy. Cilla Black, The Searchers and of course The Beatles often gave the fans their local material and in October 1963 it was Gerry and the Pacemakers' turn when for four weeks the guys held top spot with their version of *You'll Never Walk Alone*.

A song for all occasions

During that month the Kop adopted the song, taking the lyrics literally as to underline the affection they held for a team coming out of a barren spell and into one of glory. The song stuck. It became Liverpool Football Club's anthem (sorry Celtic fans!). Pink Floyd recorded the Kop in full swing and used it on their 1971 track, *Fearless*.

The anthem has become part of the fabric of Anfield and the club. Played as the team takes to the field over the speakers but, more importantly, sung by fans through the good and the bad times.

It appeared on the Shankly Gates when they opened in 1982, it now appears on the club crest, and as Liverpool fans will tell you when they're paying due respect to Fernando Torres, their Spanish hero had it on a captain's armband he wore whilst at Atletico Madrid.

The song has helped in times of adversity. After the

Hillsborough disaster in 1989 the words took on an extra poignancy, it was so memorably sung by a choirboy at the memorial service held in the City just weeks after the tragedy and many will recall AC Milan fans, just days after events in South Yorkshire, spontaneously singing the lyrics before a European Cup semi-final at their San Siro stadium.

Players who come to play for the club, be they from Bootle or Bilbao, will testify to its powers. The set of players who found themselves sitting in an Istanbul dressing-room in 2005 at half-time, 3-0 down and staring into the abyss of embarrassment, will tell you that the sound of the fans still singing their song (never have the words meant so much!) whilst not acting as some Hollywood-scripted catalyst for glory, did give them some hope that maybe, just maybe, all was not lost.

What Rogers and Hammerstein would have made of their song's new home, who knows? They were music men though who knew what a song could do for the likes of Fred Astaire, Ginger Rogers and Gene Kelly. Surely then they would have been proud that their tune, sung with more passion than any leading man or lady, had the same galvanising effect on Liverpool's many star performers.

Gerry Marsden led an emotional rendition at Anfield on the 20th anniversary of Hillsborough

HONOURS AND RECORDS

MAJOR HONOURS
LEAGUE CHAMPIONSHIP
18 times: Joint English record
1901, 1906, 1922, 1923, 1947,
1964, 1966, 1973, 1976, 1977, 1979,
1980, 1982, 1983, 1984, 1986,
1988, 1990

EUROPEAN CUP/CHAMPIONS LEAGUE
5 times: British record
1977, 1978, 1981, 1984, 2005

UEFA CUP WINNERS
3 times: British record
1973, 1976, 2001

FA CUP WINNERS
1965, 1974, 1986, 1989, 1992,
2001, 2006

LEAGUE CUP WINNERS
7 times: English record
1981, 1982, 1983, 1984, 1995,
2001, 2003

EUROPEAN SUPER CUP WINNERS
3 times: British record
1977, 2001, 2005

CHARITY SHIELD WINNERS
1964*, 1965*, 1966, 1974, 1976,
1977*, 1979, 1980, 1982, 1986*,

1988, 1989, 1990, 2001, 2006
(* Shared)

OTHER TROPHIES

- Football League Second Division Champions: 1894, 1896, 1905, 1962
- **Lancashire League Champions: 1893**
- Super Cup Winners: 1985/86
- **FA Youth Cup Winners: 1996, 2006, 2007**

RUNNERS-UP

- Football League Division One: 1899, 1910, 1969, 1972, 1974, 1975, 1978, 1985, 1987, 1989, 1991
- **Premier League: 2002, 2009**
- FA Cup: 1914, 1950, 1977, 1988, 1996
- **Football League Cup: 1978, 1987, 2005**
- European Cup: 1985, 2007
- **European Cup Winners' Cup: 1966**

INDIVIDUAL AWARDS

- Football Writers' Footballer of the Year: 1974 Ian Callaghan, 1976 Kevin Keegan, 1977 Emlyn Hughes, 1979 Kenny Dalglish, 1980 Terry McDermott, 1983 Kenny Dalglish, 1984 Ian Rush, 1988 John Barnes, 1989 Steve Nicol, 1990 John Barnes, 2009 Steven Gerrard
- **PFA Player of the Year: 1980 Terry McDermott, 1983 Kenny Dalglish, 1984 Ian Rush, 1988 John Barnes, 2006 Steven Gerrard**
- PFA Young Player of the Year: 1983

Ian Rush, 1995 Robbie Fowler, 1996 Robbie Fowler, 1998 Michael Owen, 2001 Steven Gerrard
- **Manager of the Year: Bill Shankly 1973; Bob Paisley 1976, 1977, 1979, 1980, 1982, 1983; Joe Fagan 1984; Kenny Dalglish 1986, 1988, 1990**

CLUB RECORDS

- Most points in a season: (2 points for a win) 68, 1978-79; (3 points for a win) 90, Division One 1987-88
- **Most League wins in a season: 30, Division One, 1978/79**
- Most consecutive unbeaten league games: 31, 4th May 1987 – 16th March 1988
- **Most consecutive unbeaten home games: 85, 21st January 1978**
- **– 31st January 1981**
- **Most league goals in a season: 106, Division 2, 1895/96**
- Most home league goals in a season: 68, Division 2, 1961/62
- **Most away league goals in a season: 42, Division 1, 1946/47**
- Record win: 11-0 v Stromsgodset Drammen, 17th September 1974
- **Record league win: 10-1 v Rotherham Town, 18th February 1896**
- Biggest FA Cup win: 9-0 v Newtown, 29th October 1892
- **Biggest League Cup win: 10-0 v Fulham, 23rd September 1986**
- Record defeat: 1-9 v Birmingham, 11th December 1954

INDIVIDUAL RECORDS

- Most appearances: Ian Callaghan, 857, 1960-1978
- **Most League appearances: Ian Callaghan, 640, 1960-1978**
- Most FA Cup appearances: Ian Callaghan (right), 79, 1960-1978
- **Most League Cup appearances: Ian Rush, 78, 1980-1987 & 1988-1996**
- Most European appearances: Jamie Carragher, 129, 1997-.
- **Most goals (total): Ian Rush, 346, 1980-1987 & 1988-1996**
- Most League goals: Roger Hunt, 245, 1959-1969
- **Most FA Cup goals: Ian Rush, 39, 1980-1987 & 1988-1996**
- Most League Cup goals: Ian Rush, 48, 1980-1987 & 1988-1996
- **Most European goals: Steven Gerrard, 32, 1998-**
- Most goals in a season: Ian Rush, 47, 1983/84.
- **Most league goals in a season: Roger Hunt, 41, 1961/62**
- Most hat-tricks: Gordon Hodgson, 17, 1926-1935
- **Oldest player: Ned Doig 41, 41 years, 165 days, 11th April 1908**
- Youngest player: Jack Robinson, 16 years, 250 days, 9th May 2010
- **Oldest goalscorer: Billy Liddell, 38 years, 55 days, 5th March 1960**
- Youngest goalscorer: Michael Owen, 17 years, 143 days, 6th May 1997
- **Most consecutive games: Phil Neal, 417, 23rd October 1976 - 24th September 1983**

- Record signing: Fernando Torres, £22 million from Atletico Madrid, July 2007
- **Record sale: Robbie Fowler, £12.5 million to Leeds, November 2001**

ATTENDANCE RECORDS AT ANFIELD

- Highest League attendance: 58,757 v Chelsea, Division One, 27th December 1949
- **Highest FA Cup attendance: 61,905 v Wolverhampton Wanderers, 2nd February 1952**
- Highest League Cup attendance: 50,880 v Nottingham Forest, 12th February 1980
- **Highest European attendance: 55,104 v Barcelona, 14th April 1976**
- Highest average attendance: 49,224, 1976/77
- **Lowest attendance: 1,000 v Loughborough, 7th December 1895**
- Lowest average attendance: 2,707, 1892/93

MISCELLANEOUS

- Ian Rush's five FA Cup final goals is an all-time record.
- **The Welshman scored 44 FA Cup goals (38 for Liverpool) making him the competition's second highest all-time scorer. Henry "Harry" Cursham of Notts County scored 49 between 1877 and 1888.**
- Robbie Fowler's hat-trick against Arsenal in August 1994 was scored in 4 minutes and 33 seconds and is

the fastest in Premier League history.

- **Steven Gerrard is Liverpool's most capped player, winning 80 caps for England.**
- Liverpool were the first English team to have a shirt sponsor when, in 1979, they sported Japanese electrical firm Hitachi's logo on their famous red shirts.
- **Liverpool were the first (2001) and last (2006) club to win the FA Cup while it was held at Cardiff's Millennium Stadium.**
- Liverpool played in the first FA Cup final watched by a reigning Monarch. In 1914, King George V saw Burnley beat the Reds at Crystal Palace.
- **In 2008/09, Liverpool became the first team not to win the league having lost only two matches.**
- Anfield was the first stadium shown by *Match of the Day*. In August 1964, the BBC sent their new programme to film the Champions play Arsenal. Roger Hunt scored the first goal in a 3-2 win.
- **Liverpool were the first British club to retain the European Cup, winning the trophy back-to-back in 1977 and 1978.**
- Gerrard Houllier is the only Liverpool manager to do the double over Manchester United and Everton in the same season (2001/02).
- **Liverpool striker Albert Stubbins is the only footballer to appear on The Beatles'** *Sgt Pepper's Lonely*

Hearts Club Band **album cover.**

- On their way to the treble in 2000/01, Liverpool became the first team to play in every possible game in a season. The Reds played 63 times.
- **Liverpool were the first team to get eight different goalscorers on the score-sheet in a league game when they beat Crystal Palace 9-0 in September 1989.**